T0277233

Cambridge Elements ≡

Elements in Philosophy and Logic
edited by
Bradley Armour-Garb
SUNY Albany
Frederick Kroon
The University of Auckland

LOGIC AND INFORMATION

Edwin Mares
Te Herenga Waka – Victoria University of Wellington

CAMBRIDGE
UNIVERSITY PRESS

CAMBRIDGE
UNIVERSITY PRESS

Shaftesbury Road, Cambridge CB2 8EA, United Kingdom

One Liberty Plaza, 20th Floor, New York, NY 10006, USA

477 Williamstown Road, Port Melbourne, VIC 3207, Australia

314–321, 3rd Floor, Plot 3, Splendor Forum, Jasola District Centre,
New Delhi – 110025, India

103 Penang Road, #05–06/07, Visioncrest Commercial, Singapore 238467

Cambridge University Press is part of Cambridge University Press & Assessment,
a department of the University of Cambridge.

We share the University's mission to contribute to society through the pursuit of
education, learning and research at the highest international levels of excellence.

www.cambridge.org
Information on this title: www.cambridge.org/9781009466752

DOI: 10.1017/9781009466745

First published 2024

A catalogue record for this publication is available from the British Library.

ISBN 978-1-009-46675-2 Hardback
ISBN 978-1-009-46673-8 Paperback
ISSN 2516-418X (online)
ISSN 2516-4171 (print)

Cambridge University Press & Assessment has no responsibility for the persistence
or accuracy of URLs for external or third-party internet websites referred to in this
publication and does not guarantee that any content on such websites is, or will
remain, accurate or appropriate.

Logic and Information

Elements in Philosophy and Logic

DOI: 10.1017/9781009466745
First published online: June 2024

Edwin Mares
Te Herenga Waka – Victoria University of Wellington

Author for correspondence: Edwin Mares, Edwin.Mares@vuw.ac.nz

Abstract: This Element looks at two projects that relate logic and information: the project of using logic to integrate, manipulate, and interpret information; and the project of using the notion of information to provide interpretations of logical systems. The Element defines 'information' in a manner that includes misinformation and disinformation and uses this general concept of information to provide an interpretation of various paraconsistent and relevant logics. It also integrates these logics into contemporary theories of informational updating, probability theory, and (rather informally) some ideas from the theory of the complexity of proofs. The Element assumes some prior knowledge of modal logic and its possible world semantics, but all the other necessary background is provided.

Keywords: modal logic, relevance logic, philosophy of information, information updating, probability

ISBNs: 9781009466752 (HB), 9781009466738 (PB), 9781009466745 (OC)
ISSNs: 2516-418X (online), 2516-4171 (print)

Contents

1 Logic and Information

1.1 Speed Limits and Firefighters

One day, a few years ago, my partner and I were driving along New Zealand's Highway 1 near Wellington when we were confronted with contradictory speed limit signs, as depicted in Figure 1.[1]

It seemed as if we and the other motorists were being told two incompatible things: the unique maximum speed limit on that stretch of road was 50 kilometres per hour and that the unique maximum speed limit was 70 kph.

I suggest that in this circumstance there is conflicting information. Conflicting information is a significant phenomenon in our everyday lives, and it presents the theoretical logician with interesting difficulties. These difficulties concern both how to treat the logical consequences of the information that one has and what to advise agents about how to change their information states in response to such conflicts. Sections 3 and 4 of this *Element* are about these problems, respectively.

Cases like the one given previously also illustrate important issues regarding the nature of information. First, I argue in Section 2 that having a piece of information is different from having a belief. To foreshadow this argument, in the speed limit case, we did not believe that the intended speed limit was 70 kph or that it was 50 kph. We had the information, say, that the speed limit was 50 kph, but neither of us believed that it was 50 kph. Thus, having a piece of information and believing it are distinct.

Second, the speed limit case raises an interesting normative issue. Whereas the prudential thing may have been to travel at the lower speed limit, the presence of the higher one might *entitle* my partner to drive at 70 kph. At least if she were caught going over 50 kph but below 70 kph on this stretch of road, she could argue that the presence of the 70 sign did entitle her to do so. Consider the following rather similar case. Suppose that you are shopping and find a product with two price stickers. You take it to the counter and argue that you should pay the lower of the two prices. The presence of the lower price in this case (given certain consumer laws and conventions) entitles you to pay the lower price. You might even believe that the lower sticker was put on by mistake, but that does not remove the entitlement. The information that the product has this lower price generates this entitlement.

I do not give a theory of informational entitlements of this sort. Doing so would force us to take detours into the philosophy of law and ethics and away from logic. What I do look at is two ways in which the topics of information

---

[1] As photographed on a phone through a dirty windscreen. Photo by the author.

Figure 1 Highway 1 outside Wellington

and logic interact. I look at ways in which logic can help us treat information. Sections 3 and 5, in particular, are about what logic can do for information. They talk about how different logical systems can help us organise information and how logical techniques can tell us how to update our information states in response to new information. In addition, theories of information can help us understand problems in the philosophy of logic. In Section 3, I look at using ideas from the theory of information to interpret logical systems, such as Kleene's 3-valued logics, the logic of first-degree entailments (FDE), and relevant logic. In Section 4, I use the theory of information states developed in this Element to treat the way in which we learn (or information is conveyed) through logical derivations.

Here is a similar sort of case due to Michael Dunn [28]. Suppose that you are in a hotel room and you hear the fire alarm sounding. You exit your room to see two firefighters one closer to you than the other. Firefighter 1 is pointing to your left and says 'Go this way (down a staircase). It is the only way out'.

Firefighter 2 is pointing to a staircase on your right and says the same thing. The firefighters case raises other interesting issues.

Like the speed limit case, you have to make a decision concerning on what information you are going to use as a basis for your actions. In the speed limit case, one would usually merely travel at 50 kph or less and know that they were avoiding trouble in so doing. In firefighters case, however, one does not have a natural solution of this sort. Suppose, however, you see that one of the firefighters has a book in his pocket and the title of this book is *Terrorist Manual, Volume II: The Use of Disinformation to Increase Harm*. Seeing this would prompt you to **update** your information state and remove the direction that this alleged firefighter is pointing towards as a means of escape. This shows that information, in the sense that I am using it in this Element, is *defeasible*. Section 5 treats updating information both defeasibly and non-defeasibly.

1.2 What Is Information? Preliminaries

Consider the difference between the case of the two speed limit signs and the following scenario. One night, some drunken students painted a crossing in the middle of a tunnel in Wellington. One end of the crossing ran up against a wall and so it was a crossing to nothing. But there was no real sense in which the painting presented us with the information that there was an official crossing in this tunnel. The painting work, as a consequence of the students' state of inebriation, was very sloppy and would fool no one. Unlike the case with the speed limit signs, which looked official, there was no appearance that the crossing was *grounded* in the right sort of facts that make a series of white stripes on a road into an official crossing. This *appearance of grounding*, on my view, is what is essential to the notion of information.

A piece of information is grounded if it has the relationship to a fact (a 'truthmaker') such that it is made true by that fact. One might wonder why I require that pieces of information merely appear to be grounded rather than be actually grounded. I admit that there is an important problem with taking the salient property of information that it appear to be grounded. What appears to be grounded to one person, might not appear to be grounded to another. This sort of subjectivity can cause problems in determining what is a particular agent's information state at a particular time. But getting rid of this subjectivity comes with other costs. In Sections 2 and 6 I discuss the grounding relation.

One way to make the notion of information more objective is to require as Luciano Floridi [32] does that information always be true. Then what counts as information is not agent relative in the way that I suggest. But Floridi's notion of information eschews disinformation and misinformation. I think that some of the most important reasons for analysing information using logic are to show how logical methods can be used to help eliminate misinformation and disinformation from one's information state.[2]

The issue of the subjectivity of information is rather complex. Some authors think of information as something that we possess in a rather literal sense. Information might be something contained in a database, in a notebook, or even in someone's mind. Others, such as Jon Barwise and John Perry [9], think of the information that is available to an agent as contained in his or her environment.

I agree with Barwise and Perry that the notion of an information state has to include one's environment as well as what is in his or her mind or in a particular database. Many of us keep information in various locations in our environments. I keep all my appointments (or try to) in the calendar in my university email program. I keep the receipts I use for tax purposes in an envelop or in my email inbox. I keep lists of family birthdays in a notebook. And so on. All of these elements of my information state are representational. But, in a very straightforward sense, I also possess a lot of information in a non-representational manner. Facts themselves, if they are available to me, can count as information. As I write this, I see my dog in her bed taking a nap. The fact that I perceive is information that is available to me. As J.J. Gibson [37] says, this sort of information is available to us perceptually in our environment.

1.3 Information Conditions versus Truth Conditions

Throughout this Element, I talk about the *information conditions* for statements. The notion of an information condition is very closely related to the truth condition of a statement but is importantly different.

This distinction is clearest perhaps when we talk about universally quantified statements [57]. In a Tarskian model for classical logic, a universal statement such as 'All the neighbourhood dogs are in the park' is true if and only if in the model every object o in the domain satisfies the open formula $N(x) \supset P(x)$. In other words, the Tarskian truth condition of 'All the neighbourhood dogs are in the park' is true if and only if every neighbourhood dog is in the park. This is a clear instance of the disquotational nature of truth conditions.

General information is very different from a truth condition of this sort. One might see each dog – Sadie, Nova, Milo, and so on – in the park and not realise that every neighbourhood dog is in the park. Something else is required. As Bertrand Russell [79] points out, what one needs to know is that this list of dogs is the list of all the dogs from the neighbourhood.

In order to capture this aspect of universal statements, Russell adds general facts to his ontology. I doubt that general facts are needed as truthmakers

---

[2] I think this now. In my book [55], I accepted the view that all information is true.

for statements. General information of this kind, however, is needed in order to explain how individuals have access to general truths about their environments. Such general information, however, is not mysterious (as the notion of a general fact may be). I have lived in this neighbourhood for years, and am there much of my time. I see people walking their pets and have gotten to know their dogs quite well. I bring this background with me and it is part of the environment and, together with each individual dog's being there, constitutes the information condition for 'All the dogs in he neighbourhood are in the park'.

Throughout this Element I discuss the information conditions associated with the various logical operators.

1.4 Information States

Another key concept in this Element is of an *information state*. Information states are states of agents – an information state is the information that the agent has in their possession at a given time. What is meant by 'possession' here is rather loose. I follow most of the philosophers of information in taking the way in which one holds their information to be either internal or external to their brains. The view that an information state can be (at least in part) external to the agent is akin to the *extended mind* hypothesis. The extended mind hypothesis of Andy Clark and David Chalmers [18] claims that the mind does not exclusively reside in the body, that one's memories, say, can reside in computers, note pads, and so on, outside of his or her body. One can have just as ready access to information that is represented in a computer's database as information that is remembered.

Our information states can change radically over time. Our environment changes and we sometimes we forget or lose old information. In Section 5, I discuss the application of dynamical logical methods to track the way in which information states change and are updated.

Modelling information states is crucial to the understanding of the relationship between logic and information, but the nature of such states is far from straightforward. One problem is about the coherence of information states. Suppose that an information state i contains two pieces of information. Does it contain their conjunction? For example, when I saw the two speed limit signs did I have the information that the speed limit was both 70 kph and 50 kph? Or did I merely have the information that it was 70 kph and the information that it was 50 kph? The principle of inference being questioned here is the rule of adjunction, namely,

$$\frac{i \vDash A \quad i \vDash B}{i \vDash A \wedge B} .$$

The rule of adjunction is quite important. We use adjunction to conglomerate information to make inferences. Getting rid of adjunction altogether produces a logic that is extremely weak and of little use. There are systems, such as Peter Schotch and Ray Jennings's forcing logic [81], that allow one to make conjunctive inferences from consistent sets of information. Although these systems are formally interesting, they do share a problem. We often infer information from conflicting sources and then forget where pieces of information come from. Forcing allows us to conglomerate such pieces of information as long as they do not conflict with one another. Thus, it allows us at times to use information from conflicting sources. It seems just as reasonable to use a logic that allows us to conjoin information that has explicit conflicts. (In Section 3, I examine discussive logic, which is non-adjunctive, and construct a simple modification of its semantics that makes it adjunctive.)

Another issue has to do with the metaphysics of information states. Information is propositional – it tells us something about the world. Are information states merely sets of propositions? In Section 4 I argue that what are called 'structured propositions' are involved in information states, but in Section 3 I give reasons why an information state should largely be thought of as a set of *indices*. An index, in the sense used in semantics, is a point at which a statement can be evaluated as true or false. Some examples of indices as used in semantic theories are possible worlds, times, events, and situations. A semantics that uses indices is called an 'indexical semantics' or a 'pointed semantics'. I discuss various choices of indices for a semantics of information in Section 3.

There are two aspects to the logical analysis of information states. The first one might be called the *static* aspect. The static logic is a theory of the logical principles under which the information contained in a state is closed. For example, if a state contains the information that A and the information that $A \rightarrow B$ ('A implies B'), then the logic might dictate that the state also contains the information that B. As I explain in Section 3, this closure principle is natural under certain interpretations of implication (and hence in certain logical theories) but not on other interpretations. The choice of a static logic is important for a theory of information because it, in part, determines what information is considered to be available to agents.

The second aspect is the *dynamic* aspect. The dynamic logic of information states determines the way in which states should be updated with respect to new information. The dynamic theory that I investigate in Section 5 is a modification of the dynamic epistemic logics of Johan van Benthem, Alexandru Baltag, and Sonja Smets. It combines elements from standard epistemic logics with elements from the sort of dynamic logic used to analyse computer programs. On the semantical theory, an information state is a set of indices. When a piece of new information that is consistent with the existing state is added, this set shrinks to include only those indices in the old state that make true the new information. What is more interesting is what happens when information that is inconsistent with the old state is added. I discuss this issue at length in Section 5.

1.5 Plan of the Element

The purpose of this Element is both to introduce readers to the field of the logic of information and to pursue a particular theory in this field. In this book, I try to cover the mainstream theories: the Carnap-Bar Hillel theory of the quantity of information, Dretske's theory of information content, Floridi's definition of information, situation semantics, Barwise and Seligman's channel theory, the use of dynamic logic to understand updating and revising information states, and the use of complexity theory to understand information in logical proofs. But, I have used being asked to write this book also as an opportunity to revise my old views on logic and information in my book, *Relevant Logic* [55], and produce a theory based on relevant logic and its semantics. This attempt to construct a theory is a theme that ties this Element together (especially Sections 3, 5, and 6).

In Section 2, I attempt to define information as propositions that appear true in a context. I use Luciano Floridi's definition of information as true, well-formed data as a foil, criticising the various aspects of it to motivate the definition I take. In particular I claim that there is false information. In this, I side with Michael Dunn and oppose Floridi, Grice, Barwise and Seligman, and many others. In Section 3, I look at ways in which to model information (in particular its static aspects), and pay special attention to models that allow inconsistent information. I examine possible world semantics, closed set semantics, the four-valued Dunn-Belnap semantics, and the ternary relation Routley-Meyer semantics for relevant logic.

In Section 4, I look at ways to understand the quantity of information in logical truths and increases in information that occur when proving theorems. In order to understand the nature of the information involved, I appeal to the distinction between implicit and explicit information. Implicit information is understood in terms of unstructured propositions – propositions as sets of situations. Explicit information is understood in terms of structured propositions – propositions that have individuals and properties as constituents. I think of a proof as the extraction of explicit information from premises. The difficulty of the proof (as measured by the complexity of the proof) is a measure of the amount of information in the proof. This is what I call an 'upstream' measure of information. A downstream measure is one that measures the difficulty of integrating a proposition into one's beliefs – the degree to which an agent would have to change their beliefs or other mental states rationally to accept that proposition as a belief.

Section 5 examines the dynamic aspect of information. When new information is integrated into an agent's information state, sometimes changes need to be made. I develop semantics of straightforward updating and defeasible updating that are based on the ternary relation semantics discussed in Section 3. In Section 6, I look at the Carnap-Bar Hillel (CBH) theory of information. CBH is based on a set of worlds and a probability function on those worlds. The virtues of this theory are discussed, and it is given an interpretation in terms of physical probability. CBH is also generalised to fit with almost any non-classical logic, including relevant logic. I discuss the prospect of making the connection between probability and information stronger, that is, by taking probabilities as guides to information. This idea, at least in its simplest form, is rejected.

2 What Is Information?

2.1 Introduction

In order to understand how information theory and logical theory can be made to help one another, we first need to have a workable concept of information. Although I have discussed the notion of information in the introductory section, a lot more work needs to be done before we have a useful concept. In characterising the notion of information, Michael Dunn says:

> The sense of information I have in mind can be nicely contrasted to knowledge. Plato [thought of] knowledge to be something like 'justified true belief.' Then information is what is left of knowledge when one takes away belief, justification, and truth. Of course we commonly speak of someone having information to mean it as a kind of success (truth) but this can be shown to be a mere conversational implication by the fact that we can say of a person that she has false information. Information in the sense I mean it is not even mere opinion, for that requires at least some weak sense of belief. 'She had the information all the time, but she didn't believe it at all.' Information is meant here as a kind of semantic content – the kind of thing that can be expressed by language. [25, p 423]

I have in mind a notion of information something like Dunn's, although I think there is a notion of justification at play with information. I have already said that what counts as information always appears to be true. The notion of appearance that is involved here is somewhat tricky, and is discussed at length in Section 2.7.

I discuss the relationship between information and truth in Section 2.6. I make more of an argument there concerning the separation of information and truth but my point is essentially pragmatic. Logic is useful in helping to distinguish between what is true and what is false. To remove falsehoods from the subject matter from the outset is to reduce the usefulness of the logic of information. This justification needs refinement, and receives it in Section 2.6, but the upshot is that I include false forms of information – misinformation and disinformation – in the concept of information.

Consider the case of someone who says that they could not believe what they were seeing. This sort of claim is often hyperbole, but it is not nonsensical. We often have information at hand but either do not pay enough attention to it or find it strange enough that we do not enter it into our belief set. In Section 1.4, I present the notion of an information states, which is a collection of propositions that are available as a resource to an agent, regardless of whether they believe any of these propositions. I develop this idea further in Section 2.4, and it plays an important role in the logical theories outlined in the subsequent sections of this Element.

Dunn's negative characterisation interprets the ordinary concept information in terms its relationship to an agent. Mariacarmen Martinez and Sebastian Sequoiah-Grayson look instead at theoretical approaches to information [61]. They distinguish three approaches to information in the logical literature, and I find their taxonomy quite useful. The first is the notion of *information as range*. This notion of information is the one implemented in the CBH theory discussed in Sections 3 and 6 and Johan van Benthem's theory of informational updates, discussed in Section 5. The idea is that the information carried by a proposition has to do with possibilities that are ruled out if that proposition is true.

The second notion of information they call *information as correlation*. This approach to information stems from Shannon and Weaver's theory of communication [85], and is developed in different ways by Fred Dretske [23] and Barwise and Perry [9]. On the information as correlation approach, information supervenes on a base of regularities present in nature. As I write this sentence, I have the information that it is raining outside of my house. This information comes to me by means of my sight and hearing. I can be said to have this information only because my sight and hearing deliver sensations by being a part of a reliable causal network. I adopt aspects of the information as correlation approach in the present section and Section 3.

The third approach to information is the idea of *information as code*. On this approach, the way in which one has access to information is largely by extracting it from encoded data. A logical inference is understood as this process of extraction. We find this approach to information in van Benthem [89], and Francesco Paoli's approach to proof theory [66]. The information as code approach plays an important role in Section 4.

I attempt in this section to set out a single conception of information that can be understood as the basis for each of these three approaches as taken up in the various sections of this Element.

2.2 Floridi's Concept of Information

I begin by presenting an attempt at a definition of 'information' due to Luciano Floridi [30, 32]. Floridi distinguishes the concept of semantic information from the notion of a signal and the notion of a plan for how things should be. I set aside these other notions in this Element, and like Floridi concentrate on semantic notions of information.

A semantic concept of information takes information to be about the way the world is. Floridi's definition of semantic information has four clauses. I place them in a text box in order to emphasise them. They play very significant roles in the structure and content of this section.

Definition 2.1 (Floridi's Special Definition of 'Information'). σ *is information if and only if*
(SDI.1) σ is constituted by n data *(for some $n \geq 1$);*
(SDI.2) each of these data are well-formed;
(SDI.3) each of these data are meaningful;
(SDI.4) each of these data are true.

[30, p 46]

The notion of data is central in this definition, but the word 'data' is used in a plethora of ways in the literature. Sometimes, but not always, it is only used to indicate truths. Usually, although not always, it is a syntactic notion (it is syntactic in Floridi), but not always. I think Floridi uses it to indicate what can be inserted into a database – a sentence like entity (something that is syntactic, perhaps encoded), but not necessarily true. I discuss the issue of the nature of data further in Section 2.3. Floridi's general definition of information is the same as this special definition, except that it does not include SDI.4 – the stipulation that all information is true. I return to this issue in Section 2.6, but we can already see the reason Floridi needs it (or something like it). For Floridi, a datum is a sentence in a database (or a human brain). In order to count as information, surely it needs some sort of real connection to what it is supposed to be about. If data are all true, then they are linked in a strong way to the world.

Although I do not adopt Floridi's definition, I use it as a foil for the notion that I do accept. I unpack the four concepts that appear in Floridi's definition and these can guide us to a much more useful definition.

I begin with the idea that information has to be 'well-formed'. In saying that information has to be well-formed requires that a piece of information is a *syntactic* entity of some sort. To say that something is well-formed is to say that it obeys the rules of a grammar. Cats, dogs, trees, and planets do not conform to or fail to conform to the rules of any grammar. They just are. Phrases and especially sentences are either grammatical or ungrammatical. It makes some sense to claim that information is a syntactic notion. After all, information is about things. Cats, dogs, trees, and planets are not about anything, but sentences and phrases are about things.

There is, however, an alternative to the claim that information is syntactic. A sentence typically is said to have a content, which in turn is also about the world. The content of a sentence is a *proposition*, which is language neutral. For example, I just heard that Liverpool beat Villarreal in football yesterday. Someone in Spain might have heard the same thing as I did, but heard it in Spanish. It is natural to say that we both had the same information, but it was encoded for us in two different languages. I look at the nature of propositions in more depth in Section 2.4 and in Section 4.

2.3 Information and Data

Floridi characterises information as data. But what are data? In much popular media and scientific literature, especially in computer science, data are often described as a syntactic or linguistic constructs. But sometimes it is treated as something that is extra-linguistic. On the other hand, 'data' is sometimes used to describe the facts on which a statistical inference is based. Clearly, Floridi thinks of data as syntactic, since he talks of them as obeying grammatical rules. To this extent, Floridi's notion fits within the 'information as code' approach outlined in Section 2.7.

There is, however, a problem with treating information as data. The following argument is due to Ruth Nelson [64] and Gerard Allwein [2]. Suppose that there is a secret hidden somewhere on a computer's hard disk. And suppose that the secret is somehow leaked. What does it mean to say that it has leaked? The answer to this question cannot be merely that someone who is not supposed to be in possession of the secret now has the bits with which the secret is represented in the machine. If the secret is encoded, then having the bits alone is not good enough to inform this person of the secret. Now suppose that the person also has the encryption key for that secret. This still might not be enough. The secret might be the answer to a question. After decrypting the original bits and finding the answer 'yes' the person may still not be informed of the secret, since he still does not know to what question it is an answer. There seems in this case to be well formed and true data, but it doesn't yet count as information.

Floridi might reply that 'yes' by itself is not meaningful. The people who found the 'yes' on the hard disk have no idea what proposition is being affirmed, so it is not meaningful to them. But the 'yes' is meaningful in the sense that in the context in which it was encoded it did express a proposition.

One way to avoid the sort of relativity that seems implicit in the syntactic treatment of information is to identify information with its content, that is, with propositions. In this case finding 'yes' on the hard disk does not change the state of information of the hackers investigating the hard disk in any important way, because they do not have access to the proposition that it asserts. It is one of the virtues of information-theoretic semantics that it allows us to talk about the information that is available to different people. Treating a piece of information as a proposition allows us to think of the content of information as objective.

2.4 Information and Meaning

Now that I have committed myself to holding that pieces of information are propositions, I need to make clear what I mean by 'proposition'. There are various items in the metaphysics literature that are claimed to be propositions and are claimed to be the contents of thoughts or statements. In the philosophy of mind, the key debate about propositional content is about whether thoughts have 'wide' or 'narrow' content, that is, whether contents are determined by the physical or external circumstances of the agent. We could engage in this debate too with regard to information. With regard to information, we can avoid this debate by claiming that both sorts of information are available to agents, but that the way in which they are available differs between the two sorts of content. We have more direct access to narrow content, and some of the wide content available to us we have to indicate using devices such as indexical expressions, like 'here', 'now', and 'that'.

From the perspective of what I discuss in Section 4, the more important debate is between the acceptance of structured and non-structured propositions. A non-structured proposition is a set of semantic indices, such as possible worlds (see §3.3). The non-structured proposition expressed by a sentence, A, is the set of worlds in which A is true.

Unstructured propositions are useful, especially in the sorts of theories of updating information that I discuss in Section 5. But some knowledge becomes apparent when propositions are represented in particular ways. Consider an example due to Rohit Parikh [67]. The following is a standard sort of dialogue between a teacher q and a student r:

q: Do you know the factorisation of 143?
r: Not off hand.

q: Is 11 a prime?

r: (After thinking a little) Yes.

q: Is 13 a prime?

r: Yes,

q: How much is 11 times 13?

r: Let us see; 11 times 10 is 110. 11 times 3 is 33. 110 plus 33 is 143. Oh, I see.

q: Can you factorise 143 now?

r: Of course, it is 11 times 13.

r, like all of us, already knew (in some sense) that this world is in the total set of worlds, and so the set of worlds is a truth. It represents all logically necessary truths. But what happens in the course of the previous dialogue is that *r* comes to have an *explicit* representation of a logical truth. Here I am invoking a distinction between implicit and explicit information, rather like the one made by psychologists and cognitive scientists between explicit and implicit beliefs (see, e.g., [21]). An agent's implicit information is represented by unstructured propositions (or a single unstructured proposition). A piece of explicit information is represented by a structured proposition.

A structured proposition contains the elements that are denoted by the various parts of the sentence that expresses it. For example, the sentence 'Anne is faster than Bob' can be represented in a formal language by '$F(a, b)$', which in turn can represent the structured proposition

$$\langle \mathbf{F}, \langle a, b \rangle \rangle.$$

Where **F** is the property expressed by 'F'. Structured propositions represent the manner in which we are given information in a natural way.[3]

Structured propositions are extremely useful when studying problems concerning the information contained in logical or mathematical proofs. Consider the possible worlds account of logical truth. On that theory, logical truths are true at every world. Thus (if classical logic is correct), '$p \vee \neg p$', for example, just expresses the entire set of possible worlds. As I say earlier, we all know that the set of possible worlds is true since our world must be in that set, so that we all know that every logical truth is in fact true. But, for each of us, in an intuitive sense, there are logical truths that we do not in fact know. When I tell my logic students that $(p \supset q) \vee (p \supset r)$ is a logical truth of classical logic, many are surprised. My telling them this has informed them of something and

---

[3] For theories of structured propositions, see [20, 46].

what I have informed them of is not that this world is in the set of possible worlds. If, on the other hand, what is being communicated is that

$$\langle \vee, \langle \supset, \mathbf{p}, \mathbf{q} \rangle, \langle \supset \mathbf{q}, \mathbf{r} \rangle \rangle$$

determines the whole set of possible worlds, then what is being communicated is non-trivial. In Section 4, I discuss varieties of the information as code approach that can be used to analyse information of this sort.

There are, however, problems with the use of structured propositions. For example, Frege's famous puzzle about identity statements that contain two names for the same entity, such as 'Hesperus' and 'Phosphorus', illustrates that there are informative identity statements. But the sort of representation in the theory of structured propositions that I give earlier leads one to think that the sentence 'Hesperus is identical to Phosphorus' expresses the proposition $\langle =, \langle v, v \rangle \rangle$, where v is the planet Venus. In Section 4, I describe a way to avoid this problem.

2.5 Is Information Always Propositional?

Before I go on to discuss the relationship between information and truth (again) I want to defend the idea that information is propositional. An apparent counterexample is the information one finds in maps. Maps contain information. But they do not always do so in an explicitly propositional manner. A map of New Zealand, for instance, represents Auckland as being North of Wellington, but it does so by depicting a large dot with the label 'Auckland' above the dot that is labelled 'Wellington'. There is a conventional structure to maps (e.g. one in which North is depicted as up) and there is information encoded in maps. But this conventional structure is not entirely linguistic – although names are used, lines, colours, and shapes can also be used to depict geographical features. These lines, and so on, have some sort of structural similarity to the physical layout of the place.

This similarity, however, might be highly abstract. Consider, for example, a map of an urban train system, such as the London Underground. The map of the London Underground, designed originally by Harry Black, was an important achievement. It was an achievement because it was able to incorporate a very large amount of information about the relative positions of the various stations and the lines on which they sat, in an intelligible manner. But it did so at the expense of misrepresenting the distances between stations. But if people want to travel from one station to another, this map can lead them to understand which line to take and in which direction, where to change trains, and so on.

Elisabeth Camp [14] has argued that the sense in which maps represent is not primarily propositional. In particular, she claims that the way in maps represent is fundamentally *holistic*. Camp is not denying that a map as a whole can represent a proposition in the sense of a set of possible worlds. Rather, she is claiming that the representational content of a map is not best understood as being merely a set of structured propositions (in the sense of §2.4). Since I use structured propositions in my theory of information states, I am rather interested in Camp's argument.

In explaining the sort of holistic representation that one finds in maps, Camp [14] says

> Maps are integrated representational wholes, in which a single token (which may itself be complex, in combining marks from multiple 'incompatibility classes') represents how things are at a given location, and in which spatial relations among denoted object/properties are represented by the spatial relations among the constituent tokens. Because spatial relations in the map represent spatial relations in the world, moving or otherwise altering any given marker on a single map automatically updates the represented spatial relations among that denoted object/property and all of the other represented object/properties.

Moving one name or dot in a map, say, can change a huge number (perhaps an indefinitely huge number) of propositions that the map represents, and these include both positive and negative propositions. For example, on the current London Underground map one can find that to get from Waterloo to South Kensington, one needs to take the Northern Line to Embankment and then change either to the Circle or District lines. But if we move Embankment or the Circle or District lines (i.e. the yellow or green lines) in the map, it might tell us something very different and will change the directions that are recommended for a large variety of other trips.

I think, however, that we can accept the claim that maps and some other representations do not have propositions as their primary contents, without buying into a further claim that information is not propositional. Information, in the sense that is useful for logic, needs to be propositional. Logical operators and consequence relations are relations between propositions, sets of propositions, or some other structure of propositions. In Section 2.4, I set out the idea that an information state has two parts, an unstructured set of indices and a set of structured propositions. A map may help to determine an agent's unstructured state, and the propositions that they extract from it can become explicit information for them. When one asks of a map, for example, how do I get from Waterloo to South Kensington on the Underground, one is able to formulate a set of instructions (take the Northern Line to Embankment, change to the

Circle or Piccadilly and take the train to South Kensington). These instructions can be put into propositional form ('to go from Waterloo to South Kensington ...'). This querying and extraction of information makes explicit implicit information contained in the map (and in the agent's information state).

2.6 Information and Truth

One way of dealing with the problem of distinguishing between information and pseudo-information is to adopt a fairly extreme form of externalism and claim that all genuine information is true. This is the solution adopted by Floridi [30, p 48]. There is an important tradition that identifies information with true information. Paul Grice, for instance, says

> False information is not an inferior kind of information; it just is not information. [40, p 371]

And the requirement that all information be true has some important virtues. First, it avoids the problem of conflicting information. There are no true contradictions and hence, all pieces of information are true, none of them can contradict any other information. Second, this requirement enables us to give a very straightforward answer to the problem of the right relation. A piece of information has the right relation to the world if and only if it is true of the world.

These virtues, however, come at the price that epistemological externalisms always have to pay. That is, if the truth requirement is adopted then we will have to admit that we often do not know the contents of our own information states. Consider once again the case of the two speed limit signs. Suppose that there is some fact of which my partner and I were not aware that made one of these signs correct (and the other merely false). We would then have the information that, say, the speed limit was 50 kph and we would not have the information that it was 70 kph. But we still would be confused about the speed limit. The feeling of confusion (and any of our other internal mental states such as belief) would not be affected by the external relation that the proposition that the speed limit is 50 kph bears to the world. Its apparent relation with the world and that of the proposition that the speed limit is 70 kph are unaffected by this behind-the-scenes fact that determines that only the lower limit is correct.

Moreover, imposing the truth requirement merely passes the burden of dealing with conflicts of this sort on to other epistemological theories. Instead of needing a theory of information updating that treats conflicts, we would require, say, a theory of weighing evidence that does so. Thus, the virtue of avoiding this problem can be seen as being rather less important that it might seem at first.

One who adopts the requirement that only truths can be information, however, is free to distinguish between real information and pseudo-information. The latter need not be true, but must appear to be so. Thus, among pseudo-information we can include misinformation and disinformation as well as conflicting information. Thus, the disagreement between those who impose the requirement and those who reject it may be considered a merely verbal dispute.

2.7 So, What Is Information?

Although information may be false, there has to be a close relationship between information and truth. Consider again the example of the two speed limit signs. Each of them looks legitimate. They look like signs that are posted by the New Zealand Ministry of Transport for the purpose of announcing the speed limit on roads. Let's contrast that to another real example that happened last year. Some students decided it would be funny to paint a pedestrian crossing inside a tunnel in Wellington. One side of their 'crossing' was a footpath and the other side was a wall (so there was nowhere to cross to) and the lines of the crossing were crooked and sloppily painted.

This road painting did not carry the information that pedestrians were permitted to cross there. In contrast to the speed limit signs, the painting on the road did not appear to be have the right sorts of facts backing it. The speed limit signs do appear to be backed by the right sorts of decisions at the ministry, whereas the students' seem to be backed by a wrong sort of decision (the sort made by students after an evening of drinking alcohol).

Often we do not have direct access (whatever that means) to the truthmakers for information, but rather have to infer that they exist. For example, in the house where I grew up, there was a mercury thermometer attached to the outside of the kitchen window. In the morning, when I had to decide what to wear to go to school, I looked out the kitchen window at that thermometer. I relied on the correlation between the height of the mercury and the actual temperature when making that decision. Over time, I found that correlation extremely reliable.

There are two salient points here. First, there is the epistemological point: on a particular occasion I had inductive evidence that on that particular day the temperature would be as the thermometer indicated. Second, there is a point about the physical circumstances: on a particular day there was the physical causal connection between the outside temperature and the height of the mercury. The inductive background licenses the inference from the height of the mercury to the actual temperature but should we say that this, rather than the actual physical connection, constitutes the informational relationship between the temperature and the reading on the thermometer?

Let's consider a slightly different example. Suppose that a university lecturer is entering grades for a test in an online spreadsheet. She is tired – she has just spent the day marking those tests. She enters almost all of the marks correctly but makes a mistake and enters a B+ rather than a B for one of the students. The lecturer pushes a button and each student has access to their own grades. The student whose grade is a mistake thinks with good reason that he has received a B+. This is clearly a case of misinformation. The circumstances for the student are empirically indistinguishable from those in which he actually received a B+.

Here is a similar case. Let's say that in the example of the two speed limit signs, there is a driver who cannot see the 50 kph sign. In his context (his situation, as I call it in Section 3), there is only one speed limit sign. It appears to him that the speed limit is 70 kph and the facts of his situation make it seem this way and these facts license his inference to the proposition that the speed limit is 70 kph. But let's say that the 70 kph sign was put up by mistake and the speed limit is actually 50 kph. Then this agent has information in his situation that is false. But it appears true and the driver is entitled to act as though it is true.

I want to include cases like this as cases of information. The proposition that the student has received a B+ appears to be grounded in the fact that he was given a B+. This appearance of truth is what I think of as the defining mark of information. It is this, rather than the actual truth of propositions, that we have to deal with in our everyday lives. After the student sees 'B+', he is justified in acting in certain ways. This mark may push his average grade to a level that entitles him to a position in a master's programme and after seeing it may apply for that programme.

Thus far I have indicated that the appearance of truth is a sufficient condition for a proposition's being information, but is it a necessary condition? Suppose for instance that there is a light switch in one's house that almost never works. There is a loose wire in the connection between the switch and the light. But sometimes when the switch is up, a draft in the attic of the house causes the wire to be in the right place and the light goes on. In one of these rare cases, I think that despite the fact that there is a real causal connection between the switch's position and the light's being on, the switch's being in that position does not carry the information that the light is on.

My view makes what counts as information depend on one's circumstances in an interesting way. Consider again the case of the student. Let's say he is Sam. In his situation *Sam has a B+* is information. For the lecturer who taught the course, it is not information. In fact, she has access to the test paper that has 'B' on it. In the limited circumstance that includes only Sam and his immediate surroundings, the proposition is information. In a wider circumstance that includes both Sam's and the lecturer's immediate surroundings the proposition is no longer information. The fact that it is false is demonstrated by the available evidence. The proposition no longer has the appearance of truth. This means that our inferences concerning information are in some sense *defeasible*. New information can undercut old information. This notion of defeasibility is given a formal treatment in Section 3.13.

In holding that information can be false, my view is close to Dunn's (see §2.1) but opposed to Floridi's and to Barwise and Seligman [10]. In many other respects, however, my position is very close to (and has been influenced by) Barwise and Seligman. They hold that what information exists (in general) depends on objective regularities:

> Some of them are 'nomic' regularities, of the kind studied in the sciences; others, such as those relating a map to the mapped terrain, are conventional; and others are of a purely abstract or logical character. [10, p 9]

Barwise and Seligman hold that imperfectly reliable process can carry information. But they say that 'as a general rule, the more random the system the less information will flow' (ibid.).

When there are background regularities, the explanation for events can become rather routine. My old computer does not always boot-up when I push the on button, but it almost always does. I often turn it on and then, rather than sit for a boring minute waiting for it to boot, I go do something else. But when I am off in another room making a sandwich, I am licensed to infer that the computer is booting. It is this sort of inference license that is, on my view, the heart of the notion of information.

Barwise and Seligman, I think, wish to treat information flow as an objective and (by and large) mind-independent process.[4] The existence, or non-existence, of fairly reliable connections between states of the world is an objective process, but the notion of an inference license is normative and refers in an essential manner to the existence of agents. Thus, on my view, the notion of information flow has both agent-neutral and agent-relative aspects.

2.8 Dretske's Theory of Information

Before I leave the topic of defining 'information', I would like to discuss one of the best known philosophical theories of information. That is, the view of Fred Dretske's *Knowledge and the Flow of Information* [23]. Because of its influence, I place Dretske's view in a textbox:

---

[4] Van Benthem and Israel [91] read Barwise and Seligman in this way. And it fits in with the attempt in situation theory to provide a naturalised semantic theory.

On Dretske's theory, a signal x carries the information that A if and only if the conditional probability that A given r and the agent's background knowledge k is 1 and the conditional probability that A given k alone is less than 1.

On this theory, we can derive the following **Xerox principle**: If A carries the information that B (on k) and B carries the information that C (also on k), then A carries the information that C (on k). I discuss this form of transitivity and close relations in Section 3.

Dretske adopts the terminology from Shannon and Weaver [85] of signal's carrying information. A signal is an event, most commonly (in Dretske's view) an event that is perceived. Dretske takes what information is in a signal to be relative to the background knowledge (k) of the person who is being informed. This theory is an *agent-relative* theory of information. The probability used in Dretske's definition, I think, is objective physical probability – like Barwise and Seligman (see §2.7), Dretske wants a naturalised theory of information (and knowledge), that is a theory that can be explicated fully in naturalistic terms. In addition, on Dretske's view, all real information is true. If the event that A carries information that B and the event that A really occurs, then B is true.

3 Classical Logic and Its Informational Discontents

3.1 Introduction

Classical logic is the standard logic that we teach to students in universities. It is also an excellent tool to use to do mathematics. But when we represent ideas from other fields, it can be seen to be either impoverished (needing additional vocabulary, like modal operators, counterfactual conditionals, and so on) or awkward. The treatment of conflicting information, as I say in Section 1, by restricting the application of classical rules is very awkward. In the present section, I look at logical systems that can treat conflicting information in a more straightforward manner. The treatment of conflicting information is only one issue that compels us to want a non-classical theory of information. The treatment of partial information using classical logic also seems forced. And the treatment of a relation between propositions when one carries the information that the other obtains seems to require a non-classical logic.

I begin by looking at classical logic and a semantic framework – the theory of possible worlds and argue that it needs to be modified in order to act as the basis for a theory of semantic information.

3.2 Classical Logic

The standard logical system that is taught to (often unwilling) undergraduates and is used as the basis of mathematical theories such as Peano arithmetic and the standard set theories is *classical logic*. A *standard model for propositional classical logic* is a *partial* function v from propositional variables into the singleton set, $\{T\}$. This function is extended to a satisfaction predicate $\vDash_v$ defined by the following recursive clauses:

- $\vDash_v p$ if and only if $v(p) = T$;
- $\vDash_v A \wedge B$ if and only if $\vDash_v A$ and $\vDash_v B$;
- $\vDash_v A \vee B$ if and only if $\vDash_v A$ or $\vDash_v B$;
- $\vDash_v \neg A$ if and only if $\nvDash_v A$;
- $\vDash_v A \supset B$ if and only if either $\nvDash_v A$ or $\vDash_v B$.

Standard models of classical logic are complete and consistency. The consistency of classical models makes it difficult to use them to represent conflicting information. I discuss consistency in depth in 3.4.

The completeness requirement is also problematic. A model is complete if and only if it makes every formula or its negation true. The completeness requirement on models is an instance of what is known in computer science as 'the closed world assumption'. On the closed world assumption, if we fail to have positive information regarding a proposition A, then A is deemed to be false. The closed world assumption is used in interpreting the computer language Prolog when it is applied to databases. This computer language utilises a classical negation, in the sense of the standard model. If a query is made about A and no information is obtained, then $\neg A$ is returned. This form of negation is called 'negation as failure'.

The closed world assumption is counterintuitive if made about information states or databases. Consider the difference between a database in which the entry for the number of children of Smith has been left blank and one in which it says that Smith has no children. Let 'C' mean 'Smith has children'. Then if we turn both of these databases into standard models, they both satisfy $\neg C$. But really only the second database tells us that Smith does not have any children. The first database leaves open that she does have offspring.

The problem here concerns the representation of partiality. As I say in the section on the nature of information, our information about the world is almost always partial. It does not answer every yes-no query that we have. In order to represent information states of finite beings like ourselves, then, our models must be able to represent partial information.

3.3 Possible Worlds

The first method of representing partiality that I examine does not require a rejection of classical logic. Each standard model for classical logic decides on every issue in the sense that for each formula of the language it says whether it is true or false. But we can understand a model for an information state not in terms of a single standard model, but in terms of a set of standard models. Using sets of models as a semantic structure is a simple form of the *supervaluational* approach to semantics. We have a set of valuations, each of which is determined by a single model. The supervaluation V determined by this set of valuations assigns to a formula A a value T if and only if every valuation in the set assigns T to A. When all of the models in the set are classical models, every theorem of classical logic is *super-true*, that is, true on the supervaluation. Thus, for example, the law of excluded middle $A \vee \neg A$ is super-true, but, interestingly, supervaluations are not bivalent; that is, it may be that neither A nor $\neg A$ is super-true.

We can represent the core idea of the supervaluational theory of truth in a *possible worlds semantics*. A possible worlds model contains a set of possible worlds, W. Possible world semantics is a form of the indexed semantics mentioned in Section 2. Truth or falsity of formulas is *indexed* to worlds. Each possible world acts like a standard model for classical logic. A possible worlds model for classical logic is a pair $\langle W, v \rangle$ where W is a non-empty set of possible worlds and v is a function from propositional variables to subsets of W. The truth conditions for the various connectives are the same as for classical logic (§3.2) relativised to worlds. For example, the clauses for conjunction and negation are,

$w \vDash_v A \wedge B$ if and only if $w \vDash_v A$ and $w \vDash_v B$

and

$w \vDash_v \neg A$ if and only if $w \nvDash_v A$.

A formula A is valid a model if and only if it is true in every world in that model. An entailment $A_1, \ldots, A_n \vDash_v B$ is valid on a model if and only if in every world in which every premise $A_1, \ldots, A_n$ is true, the conclusion B is also true. (We can extend this definition to treat infinitely many premises, but infinitary inferences are not germane to the topic of this Element, and I omit them for the sake of simplicity.)

I use the notation '$[\![A]\!]_v$' to denote the truth set of A, that is, the set of worlds that make A true according to v (I drop the subscripted 'v' in what follows, since I do not discuss interactions of different valuations). One way of thinking of a proposition is as a set of possible worlds. I use this notion of a proposition in Section 5. One of the more influential theories of meaning that was developed in the latter half of the twentieth century was the truth-conditional theory of meaning. On the truth conditional theory of meaning, in order to understand a declarative sentence one must understand its truth conditions. One way of formalising this theory of meaning is to represent the meaning of a sentence by a proposition qua set of possible worlds.

From a formal point of view, possible worlds models are useful and elegant. The set of propositions makes up a Boolean algebra of sets – it is closed under union, intersection, and set-theoretic complement.

One important theory of information that is constructed around possible world semantics is the Carnap-Bar Hillel theory of information. Because of its importance, I present it in a text box:

The Carnap-Bar Hillel Semantic Theory of Information (CBH). The possible worlds framework is associated largely with qualitative theories of information, but Rudolf Carnap and Yehoshua Bar Hillel put forward a quantitative theory of information that employs the notion of a possible world as a central concept. Their framework uses Carnap's construction of possible worlds, or 'state descriptions' as he calls them, but I translate their theory into our framework. Assume a possible worlds model $\langle W, v \rangle$. Also assume a probability function P from the propositions determined by v into the real interval $[0, 1]$. The content of a sentence is the set of worlds at which the sentence is false [15, pp 10-11]. So, the content of A is $Cont(A) = [\![\neg A]\!]$ and the measure of the content of A is $cont(A) = P([\![\neg A]\!])$. Thus the measure of the content of a tautology is 0 and the measure of the content of a contradiction is 1. The measure of information (in) is a bit more difficult to understand. Stated formally, it is

$$in(A) = Log_2 \frac{1}{P([\![A]\!])}.$$

This means that the measure of information of a statement is the number that taken as an exponent of 2 yields the inverse of the probability of that statement. The idea is that the more difficult a statement is to confirm, the more information it contains. I discuss the numerical measures further in Section 6.

This possible world treatment of information has virtues. It is simple but mathematically quite powerful. It does have flaws as well. In particular, it treats all contradictions as representing the empty set and so cannot provide a useful analysis of conflicting information. As I argue in Sections 3.5 and 3.6, its treatment of partial information is also problematic. In the next few sections, I outline other semantics that attempt to provide more adequate treatments of conflicts and/or partial information.

3.4 Closed Set Semantics

The first attempt to treat inconsistent information that I examine is due originally to Stanisław Jaśkowski in a series of papers from the late 1940s [43, 44, 45]. On Jaśkowski's view, there are two sorts assertions accepted in a conversation – those that are accepted without reservation, and those that are accepted tentatively. The latter are accepted 'in accordance with one of the participants in the discourse' [45, p 49]. These sorts of assertions are called 'discussive assertions'. When someone in a conversation says that A but it is accepted by the other participants as a discussive assertion, it has the content 'it is possible that A' (ibid.). Accordingly, Jaśkowski's logic is a modal logic.

Jaśkowski represents his discussive theory inside a modal logic. He takes a discussive assertion to be, in effect, the assertion of a possibility. For example, the discussive assertion of A is an assertion of $\Diamond A$ ('it is possible that A'). We can represent discussive assertions in a possible worlds model by adding an *accessibility relation* on worlds. An accessibility relation is a binary relation – I use 'M' (for 'modality') – such that 'Mww'' says that w' is possible relative to w. Thus, a discussive logic model is a triple, $\langle W, M, v \rangle$. Discussive assertion can be represented in this model by a satisfaction relation $\Vdash_v$ between worlds and formulae, defined by the following recursive clauses:

- $w \Vdash_v p$ if and only if there is some world w' such that $w' \in V(p)$ and Mww';
- $w \Vdash_v A \wedge B$ if and only if $w \Vdash_v A$ and $w \Vdash_v B$;
- $w \Vdash_v A \vee B$ if and if $w \Vdash_v A$ or $w \Vdash_v B$;
- $w \Vdash_v \neg A$ if and only if there is some world w' such that Mww' and $w \nVdash_v A$.

This semantics is **paraconsistent**. This means that the semantics does not make valid the rule of explosion; that is, we cannot validly infer every formula from every contradiction according to this logic. The possibility of informational conflicts makes it reasonable to accept a paraconsistent logic of information. It is an advantage of this semantical theory is that it shows how to take any standard model for modal logic and turn it into a paraconsistent semantics. It does not require the addition of *impossible worlds* in the same way as do some other paraconsistent semantics. If one is happy to take on board possible worlds, then they should have no metaphysical qualms about adopting this semantics.

These models are often called *closed set models*. The notion of closure used here is from the mathematical field of topology. A closure operator C from sets of worlds to sets of worlds can be defined as follows:

$$C(X) =_{df} \{w : \exists w'(w' \in X \wedge Mww')\}$$

If we restrict the models that we discuss to those in which M is both reflexive (i.e. for all w, Mww) and transitive (if Mww' and $Mw'w''$, then Mww''), then we can prove that C has the following useful properties:

1. $X \subseteq C(X)$ (enclosure);
2. if $X \subseteq Y$, then $C(X) \subseteq C(Y)$ (monotonicity);
3. $C(C(X)) = C(X)$ (idempotence).

Given a closed set model, let $[A]_v$ be the set of worlds w' such that $w' \Vdash_v A$. On reflexive and transitive models, we can prove Fact 1:

Fact 1. $[A]_v = C([A]_v)$.

This fact says that every proposition on a model is a closed set of worlds.

Using this semantics to represent information, we can understand these closed set models as identifying informational content of a statement A, not with the worlds in which the A is actually true, but rather with the set of worlds in which the A appears to be grounded in the facts. Given the conception of information given in Section 2 this seems rather natural.[5]

Defining a consequence relation $\Vdash_v$ in a similar way to §3.3, yields a theory that does make explosion valid, but it does make valid the dual rule of *implosion*. For example, in every model $A \vee \neg A$ is valid in the sense that $[A \vee \neg A]_v = W$. Thus,

$B \Vdash_v A \vee \neg A$

is valid on every closed set model. This holds for any valid formula in conclusion position. This means that on the closed set semantics every proposition carries the information that every valid formula obtains. This is rather counterintuitive.[6]

---

[5] I am grateful to one of the anonymous referees for giving this interpretation of the semantics.
[6] For more about closed set logic, see [63, 29].

3.5 Partiality and Information

In discussing information, it is useful to make a distinction between *contexts of reception* and *contexts of evaluation*. I discuss contexts of reception first and then turn to contexts of evaluation.

A context of reception is a circumstance in which one finds (or fails to find) information. For example, as I sit in my office, I look around and see my books. I see that several are missing. There is a place on a shelf for Ian Hacking's *The Social Construction of What?*, but no book occupies that place. I check the Amazon site on my computer and see that I had bought a hardback copy of that book on 15 October 1999. So I have the information that I did own that book. But I have no idea where my copy of it is now.

This is partial information. The circumstances that I currently occupy do not answer the question, 'Where is my copy of *The Social Construction of What?*' The answer to that question is out there: the world as a whole contains the exact location of my copy of this book. But my current circumstances do not contain all the facts about the world.

One might object that the notion of one's current circumstances is rather vague. This is true. If I were prepared to scour the earth in search of my copy of that book, all the facts available from the earth during my lifetime could be said to make up my circumstances. This extended context, however, is still partial. It does not contain facts available only in the unremembered past, nor does it contain facts available only in other parts of the universe. If my book was stolen by aliens and is now in the delta quadrant of the galaxy, the answer to the question of where the book is located is not in any way available in my circumstances (at least not in any epistemically useful sense). Although there are perhaps infinitely many different circumstances in which one can be located, only some of them are useful in understanding one's informational state.

A context of evaluation is an index that makes up an unstructured proposition, that is, an unstructured informational content. When I think about the possibility that a particular student has borrowed but not returned my copy of Hacking's book, I am thinking about indices (such as possible worlds) at which it is true that the student borrowed my book or, on the closed set semantics given in §3.4, indices at which it appears that they have borrowed my book.

As well as the context of reception, the proposition considered is partial. It does not contain all information (it would be useless if it did). Taking a proposition to be a set of possible worlds is one way of capturing this sense of partiality. In some of those worlds the student asks my permission to borrow the book, but in others they do not. Thus, it is not part of the proposition itself that permission is asked nor is it part of the proposition that the student does not ask permission.

This means of treating partiality may not, however, be adequate. To illustrate why, I borrow an example from Patrick Allo [1, pp 667-668]. Suppose that you and I are talking on the phone. I can convey to you that I have access to a particular piece of information, by stating a tautology, $p \vee \neg p$. On the possible worlds view (and the closed set semantics) every proposition entails $p \vee \neg p$, but I am telling you that in my context of reception there is the means to discover which out of p or $\neg p$ holds. This non-trivial use of a tautology to convey information is not explained by the possible worlds treatment of propositions.

3.6 Situations

To treat the partiality of information both in contexts of reception and in propositions, I turn to Barwise and Perry's [9] situation semantics. The central idea behind situation semantics is that parts of worlds – called situations – are better suited to semantics of information than are whole worlds. My current situation contains only the facts that are manifest in my office. It does not include facts about location of my copy of the Hacking book and it does not contain the disjunctive fact that either my student borrowed my book or he did not.

A situation, in the sense that I am using the term, is an abstract object that characterises a part of the world. If the situation is accurate, it captures the facts that obtain in that part of the world, but it may be very partial. To help elucidate the idea, let us consider an argument for situations (as opposed to complete worlds) due to Angelika Kratzer [48]. A painter named Paula paints a picture of a still life, which includes some apples and some bananas. Kratzer imagines two conversations, one with a pedant and one with a lunatic. The pendant asks Paula, 'what did you do last night?' and she answers, 'All I did was paint this still life'. The pedant replies, 'That isn't all you did – you ate, drank, and breathed'. The lunatic asks the same question and receives the same answer, but replies 'That isn't all you did. You also painted each apple and each banana'. Kratzer claims that what Paula does, and what we all do, is think of the world in terms of *lumps*. She has lumped together the painting of the apples and bananas into one act or event – the painting of the still life. She also excludes things from the lump, such as the individual act of painting each piece of fruit and her breathing, eating, and drinking. If we think of a possible world, it will be impossible to exclude the other acts (such as painting each piece of fruit) from the act of painting the particular still life.

There are situation that just contains the information that Paula paints apples and bananas as a single act, but does not contain the information that there was an act in which she painted this banana, a different act in which she painted that banana, and so on. Having situations that contain only some pieces of information is quite handy in constructing a semantical theory.

I hold that both contexts of reception and contexts of evaluation are situations. Adopting situations in the semantics allows a nuanced treatment of partiality of both contexts of reception and contexts of evaluation and allows a theory of negation that allows for conflicts of information (§3.8).

One might wonder whether individual situations could be taken to be propositions. Unfortunately it is difficult to give an adequate treatment of disjunction if contents are taken to be individual situations (see §3.9), and I treat unstructured propositions as sets of situations.

In *Situations and Attitudes*, Barwise and Perry use Kleene's three-valued semantics (K_3) semantics. It can be described in the following manner. A situation model is a pair $\langle S, V \rangle$ such that S is a non-empty set (of situations) and V is a function from propositional variables to pairs of sets of situations. For a propositional variable, p, $V(p)$ is a pair $(\llbracket p \rrbracket_V^+, \llbracket p \rrbracket_V^-)$, where $\llbracket p \rrbracket_V^+$ and $\llbracket p \rrbracket_V^-$ are sets of situations. The union of $\llbracket p \rrbracket_V^+$ and $\llbracket p \rrbracket_V^-$ might not include every situation, but the two sets are not allowed to overlap. V determines a satisfaction relation $\vDash_V$ and an *antisatisfaction* relation $\dashv_V$. The antisatisfaction relation tells us which formulae are false at situations. For propositional variables, we have

$$s \vDash_V p \text{ if and only if } s \in \llbracket p \rrbracket_V^+$$

and

$$s \dashv_V p \text{ if and only if } s \in \llbracket p \rrbracket_V^-.$$

These relations are extended to treat all formulae by means of a doubly recursive definition:

Conjunction

$$s \vDash_V A \wedge B \text{ if and only if } s \vDash_V A \text{ and } s \vDash_V B$$
$$s \dashv_V A \wedge B \text{ if and only if } s \dashv_V A \text{ or } s \dashv_V B$$

Disjunction

$$s \vDash_V A \vee B \text{ if and only if } s \vDash_V A \text{ or } s \vDash_V B$$
$$s \dashv_V A \vee B \text{ if and only if } s \dashv_V A \text{ and } s \dashv_V B$$

Negation

$$s \vDash_V \neg A \text{ if and only if } s \dashv_V A$$
$$s \dashv_V \neg A \text{ if and only if } s \vDash_V A$$

This semantics allows formulae to be true, false, or neither true nor false at situations. It does not allow any formula to be both true and false in the same situation. This semantics deals well the partiality of information both in terms of contexts of reception and evaluation, but it does not treat conflicts in any useful manner.

3.7 Four-Valued Semantics

In order to treat conflicts, we could extend the semantics of Section 3.6 to allow formulae to be both true and false in the same situation. This is allowed in the four-valued semantics due originally to Dunn [27], and has been suggested as a treatment of information by Dunn [26, 28] and Nuel Belnap [11, 12].

The four-valued semantics differs only from the three-valued semantics in that $[\![p]\!]_V^+$ and $[\![p]\!]_V^-$ are allowed to overlap; that is, they might contain situations in common. On this semantics we can think of a formula as being satisfied, anti-satisfied, both satisfied and antisatisfied, or neither satisfied nor antisatisfied at a situation.

This four-valued logic has no logical truths, in the sense that there are no formulae (that contain just the conjunction, disjunction and negation vocabulary) that are satisfied in every situation in every model. But these models do determine a consequence relation. Defining the consequence relation as before, as $A_1, \ldots, A_n \vDash_V B$ if and only if in every situation in which $A_1, \ldots, A_n$ all hold according to V, B is also true. On this definition of consequence, the following inferences are valid:

$$A \vDash_V \neg\neg A$$
$$\neg\neg A \vDash_V A$$
$$A \wedge (B \vee C) \vDash_V (A \wedge B) \vee (A \wedge C)$$
$$\neg A \wedge \neg B \vDash_V \neg(A \vee B)$$

On this semantics, however, the following version of the rule of contraposition is not valid:

$$\frac{A \vDash_V B}{\neg B \vDash_V \neg A}$$

We can make this rule valid if we alter the definition of 'consequence' to say that $A \vDash_V B$ if and only if in all situations in which V satisfies A, V also satisfies B true **and** in all situations in which V antisatisfies B is false V also antisatisfies A. This definition becomes slightly more complicated when we also consider inferences with more than one premise, and it becomes much more complicated when we add an implication connective to the language and try to make the rule of contraposition true for implications [73]. For this reason, I abandon the

four-valued semantics in favour of a theory that uses an incompatibility relation
between situations.

3.8 Incompatibility

The incompatibility semantics for negation is due to Robert Goldblatt [38]. This
semantics employs an *incompatibility* relation, $\perp$, on situations. An incompatibility model is a triple $\langle S, \perp, v \rangle$ such that v is a function from propositional
variables to sets of situations. v determines a satisfaction relation $\vDash_v$ (the is no
need for an antisatisfaction relation) that obeys the same satisfaction clauses
for conjunction and disjunction as in the three- and four-valued semantics, but
has the following satisfaction clause for negation:

   $s \vDash_v \neg A$ if and only if, for all situations $t \vDash_v A$, $s \perp t$

This clause says that s satisfies $\neg A$ if and only if every situation that satisfies
A is incompatible with s.

   I find the incompatibility semantics for negative information quite intuitive.
On this semantics, one has the information that a negation, $\neg A$, holds only
when they have the information that something incompatible with A obtains.
The idea is that all information about a situation is really positive information.
For example, I can see that my table is not black because I can see that it is
brown and I know that brown and black are distinct colours.

   The semantics allows situations to be incompatible with themselves, and
hence contain inconsistent information. Also, given a formula A, there can be
situations which satisfy neither A nor $\neg A$.

   The rule of contraposition is valid on the incompatibility semantics without
any added conditions. Double negation rules, however, do require additional
condition on models. The rule of double negation introduction,

   $A \vDash_v \neg\neg A,$

can be made valid merely by stipulating that the incompatibility relation is
symmetrical, that is, if $s \perp t$ then $t \perp s$ for all situations s and t.

   The converse rule, double negation elimination,

   $\neg\neg A \vDash_v A,$

is slightly more difficult to satisfy. Here is a fix due to Richard and Val Routley
[78] and Dunn [24]. To make sense of this fix, I need first to add a *hereditariness*
relation, $\leq$, on situations. '$s \leq t$' means that all of the information is s is also
in t.

   For a situation s, let $s^{\perp}$ be the set of situations that are incompatible with s and
let s^c be the set of situations that are not in $s^{\perp}$. The set s^c is the set of situations

that are compatible with s. In order to make the principle of double negation elimination valid, the Routleys and Dunn stipulate that for every situation there is a maximal compatible situation. More formally, the condition says that for every situation s, s^c has a unique $\leq$-maximal member, s^*.[7]

3.9 Issues Concerning Disjunction

I used to have two dogs, Zermela and Lola. Often I would hear a bark, and would have the information that one of my dogs barked, but not which one had done so. So, I would not have the information that Zermela barked (Z) or the information that Lola barked (L). But I would have the information that either Zermela barked or that Lola barked ($Z \vee L$). In the semantics I present in this Element, a situation satisfies a disjunction $A \vee B$ if and only if it satisfies at least one of A or B. The idea that all disjunctions are 'resolved' in situations is somewhat counterintuitive because as the previous example shows, not all disjunctive information is resolved for us in concrete situations. If abstract situations are to be understood as abstractions from concrete situations, then it would seem that not all disjunctions should be resolved in abstract situations.

One way of dealing with unresolved disjunctions, due to Lloyd Humberstone [42], Kosta Došen [22], Hiroakira Ono [65], and Ross Brady [13], is to add an intersection operator, $\sqcap$, to the model theory. Where s and t are situations, $s \sqcap t$ is also a situation. The intersection operator is used to give a satisfaction clause for disjunction:

$s \vDash_v A \vee B$ if and only if there are situations t and u,

$t \vDash_v A$, $u \vDash_v B$, and $t \sqcap u = s$

The idea is that if $t \sqcap u = s$, then both t and u extend s and s contains just the information that is common to both t and u. The idea that situations are closed under intersection is one that I find rather intuitive. Unfortunately, the interaction between the intersection operator, the incompatibility relation, and the mechanisms used to treat implication are very complicated.

One way of avoiding the issue of unresolved disjunctions, without recourse to adding more semantic machinery, is to the distinguish between the states of affairs that are *contained* in a situation and the information that is *carried* by that situation.[8] Consider again the situation in which I hear a bark. In my

---

[7] See also [75] and [54].

[8] When I presented a talk on unresolved disjunctive information at a conference in 1996, Jon Barwise made this suggestion to me.

immediate physical surroundings there is nothing to determine what had caused the barking noise. This situation, in other words, does not by its physical contents alone determine the information that Zermela barked or that Lola barked ($Z \lor L$). It is only relative to the regularities and other informational connections associated with the situation (see §2.7) that I could be said to have the information that $Z \lor L$. The information that $Z \lor L$ is in my information state (see §3.12) but not in my situation.

The distinction between information in a situation and the information carried by a situation is extremely useful when dealing with misinformation and disinformation. Consider a famous case of disinformation during the second world war in which a dead body was dressed as a British officer and fake invasion plans were planted on him. The German intelligence officers who investigated the case, after the body washed up on a Spanish beach, had certain information in their situation. There was a body, some documents, and so on. But they had to use further informational links to infer that the documents were accurate. The accuracy of the documents, in my view, were carried by the immediate physical situation of the German officers, but was not information contained in that situation.

By accepting the distinction between containing and carrying information, I am made free to use the standard and easier semantics for disjunction. The information condition for disjunction is

$$s \vDash_v A \lor B \text{ if and only if } s \vDash_v A \text{ or } s \vDash_v B.$$

By adopting this semantic clause for disjunction, I also can adopt Allo's view that we can indicate that certain specific information is in a situation by stating a disjunction (§3.5). One can indicate that her or her resource situation resolves a disjunction by stating that disjunction. If I say to you, 'Either my copy of Hacking's book is in my office or it is not' I indicate to you that there is a way of resolving the disjunction (i.e. by turning over my office completely in search of the book).

In Section 3.10 and the remainder of the section, I discuss theories that capture the nature of the assumptions (and facts) that underpin the carrying of information.

3.10 Implication

The links between the states of affairs in one's situation and the information carried by that situation, to use the terminology of Barwise and Perry [9], are constraints of a certain sort. These constraints are imposed by the agent. As I say in Section 2, these constraints are gleaned (correctly or incorrectly) by the agent from certain regularities that appear to be in the situation. Among these are laws of nature, causal regularities, and conventions (such as those that determine the nature of a speed limit sign and its relationship to the legal speed limit).

I represent constraints as implications of the form, $A \rightarrow B$. Introducing a *connective* to express informational links can only be justified if it makes sense to have *nested* implications of this sort. A nested implication is a formula in which implications occur within the scope of other implications. For instance, in the formula $A \rightarrow (B \rightarrow C)$. I think it does make sense to think of propositions' carrying the information that informational links obtain. For example, the Academie Francaise is an institution in France that has been empowered since the seventeenth century to set out conventions for the French language. Some decades ago, they coined the term 'le courriel' for the English 'email'. Thus, if my French cousin, Robbie, tells me on the phone, 'Je tu ai envoyé un courriel', this carries the information that there is an email from her in my inbox. I represent that by a formula $p \rightarrow (q \rightarrow r)$ where p is the establishment by the Academie of the convention concerning 'courriel', q is Robbie's saying that sentence to me over the phone, and r is the email's being in my inbox. Underlying all these implications are networks of reliable causal processes – those concerning the dissemination of the edicts of the Academie, the fact that Robbie is an extremely honest person, and the email network.

3.11 Universal and Local Logics

Barwise and Seligman [10] distinguish between the universal logic of a model and the local logic determined by an agent in a situation. I adopt this distinction, but not their formal semantic framework. It contains a lot of machinery that I do not use elsewhere in this Element. Instead I employ first the framework of modal logic (and in §3.12 complicate it somewhat) to illustrate how to this distinction can be understood.

In a situation, s, an agent may have the background of certain regularities, conventions, and so on. From this perspective, certain situations seem regular to them. These are the situations that obey the implications that the agent is licensed to adopt in s. In other words, suppose that the agent is entitled to adopt $A \rightarrow B$ in s. Then, if t is normal from this perspective, and $t \vDash_v A$, then t also satisfies B. To model this notion of regularity, I add a binary relation, M_E, to the semantics ('E' here stands for 'obeying the expected rules'). Strictly speaking, I should index the relation to each of the agents in the model. But here I am not concerned with multi-agent models, so to make things simpler, I do not bother to indicate to which agent the relation belongs.

The agent's local logic in s is represented by a relation $\vDash_s$.[9] $\vDash_s$ is determined by the set of situations that are normal with respect to the agent in s. Thus, for a single-premise inference, from A to B, $A \vDash_s B$ if and only if in every situation that is normal for the agent relative to the situation s that satisfies A also satisfies B. Generalising this idea, where Γ is a set of formulae,

$$\Gamma \vDash_s A \text{ if and only if } \left(\bigcap_{G \in \Gamma} [\![G]\!] \right) \cap M_E s \subseteq [\![A]\!].$$

The expression '$M_E s$' denotes the set of situations that are expected by the agent in s. Since we are talking about human agents, it seems that only finite premise sets are of interest. Where Γ is finite, we can represent the same idea using an implication, that is

$$s \vDash \wedge \Gamma \to A \text{ if and only if } \left(\bigcap_{G \in \Gamma} [\![G]\!] \right) \cap M_E s \subseteq [\![A]\!].$$

Making this look more like standard modal logic, we have

$$s \vDash (G_1 \wedge \ldots \wedge G_n) \to A$$

if and only if

for all t such that $M_E st$, if $t \vDash G_1$ and ... and $t \vDash G_n$, then $t \vDash B$.

Where there is only one premise, the satisfaction condition for implication is just the satisfaction condition for strict implication for standard modal logic.

The relation M_E can also be used to define an agent's information state relative to a situation. Suppose that the agent is in s. In this semantics, an information state is defined as follows: The information state of an agent in s is the set of situations t such that $M_E st$ and $s \leq t$. All of the facts in s are in the agent's information state, but not all of the information in the information state may not be in s. Where 'SA' means that A is in the agent's information state, $s \vDash SA$ if and only if for all t such that $M_E st$ and $s \leq t, t \vDash A$. Thus,

$$A \to SA$$

is logically valid (i.e. true in all situations). The converse, $SA \to A$, however is not valid. This is because some of the information in the agent's state may fail to hold in their situation.

Let SA be defined as previously and EA be true in a s if and only if it is true in all situations accessible to s by the relation M_E. Then the logics of E and S are normal modal logics. The following are valid:

---

[9] I drop the subscripted 'v' for the rest of this *Element* because the notation otherwise becomes too crowded.

$$((A \to B) \wedge EA) \to EB; \quad ((A \to B) \wedge SA) \to SA;$$
$$(EA \wedge NB) \to N(A \wedge B); \quad (SA \wedge SB) \to S(A \wedge B).$$

The logic of E also has a necessitation rule; that is, where A is valid on a model in the sense of being true in every situation, EA is also valid. The same rule holds of S, but this follows directly from the fact that $A \to SA$ is also valid.

The logic of E is a paraconsistent version of the modal logic K. If we place conditions on the relation M_E, such as reflexivity, symmetry, or transitivity, then it will be a stronger logic. We can only accept reflexivity of E if we were also to accept the claim that all information is true. In his logic of the operator 'being informed that', Floridi accepts both reflexivity and symmetry [31], but his notion of information is significantly different from my own (see Section 2), and these differences affect the logic of information.

A structure of the form $\Gamma \vDash A$ is called a 'sequent'. The universal logic of a model is the set of sequents that are satisfied by the whole set of situations. Let $\vDash_{\mathfrak{M}}$ be the consequence relation of the universal logic of a model, $\mathfrak{M}$, and $\vDash_s$ be the consequence relation of a situation s in $\mathfrak{M}$. Then $\vDash_{\mathfrak{M}} \subseteq \vDash_s$; that is, every sequent that is valid in the universal logic is valid in every local logic.

Both $\vDash_{\mathfrak{M}}$ and $\vDash_s$ are transitive. They both admit standard (intuitionist) cut rules:

$$\frac{\Gamma, A \vDash_{\mathfrak{M}} B \quad \Delta \vDash_{\mathfrak{M}} A}{\Gamma, \Delta \vDash_{\mathfrak{M}} B} \qquad \frac{\Gamma \vDash_{\mathfrak{M}} B \quad B \vDash_{\mathfrak{M}} C}{\Gamma \vDash_{\mathfrak{M}} C}$$

and

$$\frac{\Gamma, A \vDash_s B \quad \Delta \vDash_s A}{\Gamma, \Delta \vDash_s B} \qquad \frac{\Gamma \vDash_s B \quad B \vDash_s C}{\Gamma \vDash_s C}$$

In the local logic, the transitivity of implication has the following form:

$$((A \to B) \wedge (B \to C)) \vDash_s (A \to C)$$

In the universal logic, it has a stronger form:

$$\frac{B \vDash_{\mathfrak{M}} C}{A \to B \vDash_{\mathfrak{M}} A \to D}$$

The universal logic also admits a weak form of the deduction theorem, that is,

$$\frac{A_1, \ldots, A_n \vDash_{\mathfrak{M}} B}{\vDash_{\mathfrak{M}} (A_1 \wedge \ldots A_n) \to B}.$$

Local logics do not in general admit either this strong form of transitivity or even this weak form of the deduction theorem.

3.12 Ternary Relation Semantics

In the binary relation semantics for implication given in Section 3.11, the formula $A \rightarrow (B \rightarrow B)$ is satisfied by every situation for any A and B. More generally, where $B \vDash_{\mathfrak{M}} C$, then $A \rightarrow (B \rightarrow C)$ holds in every situation. But this is counterintuitive. Just because a formula B might be valid, does not mean that every proposition carries the information that B, but this semantics says that it does.

In order to avoid this problem, I adopt a semantics of implication due to Richard Routley and Robert Meyer [76, 77] that employs a *ternary* relation, R, between situations. The satisfaction clause for implication on the ternary relation semantics is the following:

$s \vDash A \rightarrow B$ if and only if for all situations t, u, if $Rstu$ and $t \vDash A$, then $u \vDash B$

Treating implication in terms of a ternary relation allows situations to *fail* to satisfy as implications some or even all of the laws of the universal logic. On this semantics there can even be situations at which the implication $A \rightarrow A$ fails! (I give the full formal semantics in §3.14.)

Section 3.11 represents the notion of a normal situation relative to a situation s using a binary relation M_E. The ternary relation can be used to represent a similar concept. When $Rstu$ holds, this means that u is a *normalisation of t relative to s*. In other words, from the standpoint of s, u includes all the information that one would expect given the contents of the situation t.

This reading of the ternary relation is closely connected to the interpretation I give of it in my book *Relevant Logic* [55]. In that book, I say that $Rstu$ if and only if u contains all the information that the links present in s (such as laws of nature, conventions, and so on) allow someone to infer from the information in t. There are significant differences, however, between the theory of [55] and the present theory. In particular, the theory of that book requires that implications express perfectly reliable connections. One consequence of this difference is that the logic motivated here is weaker than the logic of that book.

The ternary relation can also be used to represent the notion of an information state. I construct the information state of an agent in a situation s as follows. The information state is the set of normalisations of s relative to s that contain s. In formal notation, $M_S st$ if and only if (1) $Rsst$ and (2) $s \leq t$. $I(s)$ is the information state of s. This means that $s \vDash SA$ if and only if, for all t in $M_S st$, $t \vDash A$.

The information state of an individual or collective agent at s contains all the information immediately given in s and the information that can be inferred from this immediately given information by those implications that are supported by s. So, the information state of an agent at s is just the normalisation of s from the standpoint of s that also includes all the information immediately given in s.

We can also use the ternary relation semantics to obtain a relativised theory of information content. Recall that on the CBH theory of information, the informational content of a statement A is the set of all worlds at which A fails to be true. In defining the content of a statement from the situated perspective, one might just take the content of A to be the set of all situations at which A fails to hold. But this notion of information seems rather divorced from the way in which people in situations convey information. When one is told that A holds, they assess it in terms of the situations that they think are somehow reasonable, not in terms of all situations.

Instead, there are two reasonable measures of content for an assertion that A from the perspective of a situation s. The content that A might be taken to be the set of normal situations relative to s in which A fails to hold or it could be the set of situations in the information state at s in which A fails to hold. If we take the latter choice, then every proposition in the information state of s will have the empty set as content. This captures the idea that we cannot be informed of anything that we already have as information.[10]

3.13 Defeasibility and Implication

Neither the binary nor the ternary relation semantics captures the notion that an agent's informational entitlements are defeasible, but further information can in some cases undermine one's inferential licenses. If it comes to light that one of the firefighters in Dunn's scenario is not actually a firefighter but rather a terrorist wearing a firefighter's uniform who wants to mislead tourists and have them burn to death, then the inference from his wearing that uniform to his being a firefighter is no longer appropriate.

To capture this sort of defeasibility, Barwise [8] suggests a version of the semantics for counterfactual conditionals that, again, employs a lot of machinery that I do not need here. Instead I examine a simple semantics for conditionals due originally to Brian Chellas [16, 17] (and see [82, 69]). This treatment of conditionals requires the addition of a set of *restricted modal accessibility relations* to the model theory. Where A is a formula, the relation M_A relates pairs of situations. I follow Chellas in adding the operator $[A]$ for

---

[10] Patrick Allo [1] constructs a very interesting theory of conditional information in the framework of the ternary relation semantics. Let A_s be the set of situations u such that there is a $t \vDash A$ and $Rstu$. Then, the information that B on the condition that A is given by the set $A_s \setminus [\![B]\!]$. This gives us the a form of informational content of the assertion that $A \rightarrow B$.

each formula of the language – this is a form of necessity operator. In order to treat necessity operators of this form, I add to the definition of a model a set of propositions, *Prop*, such that $[\![A]\!]$ is in *Prop* for every formula A. Corresponding to each formula A, is an accessibility relation $M_{[\![A]\!]}$. In what follows, I write 'M_A' instead, for ease of reading.

The restricted necessity operator is given a satisfaction condition in terms of the corresponding relation:

$$s \vDash [A]B \text{ if and only if for all } t, \text{ if } M_A st, \ t \vDash B$$

In [59], André Fuhrmann and I give the formula $[A]B$ the reading 'given the background conditions assigned to A, B'. Let's suppose that s is the situation in which the agent finds themself in the burning hotel with the two people dressed as firefighters. Let F_1 express the proposition that person one's being dressed as a firefighter implies that he is a firefighter and similarly for F_2 and person two. Thus, in s, F_1 is assigned to statements such as 'there is someone in the hallway dressed as a firefighter'.

Now consider a situation s' similar to s in which the agent finds out, say, that person one is a terrorist. Then F_1 is undermined does not hold in s'. The additional information that one of the firefighters is a terrorist changes what is considered standard: new information may change what one thinks is standard!

A logic of relevant counterfactuals that combines the ternary relation with this binary relation is constructed by Fuhrmann and myself in [59]. There we define the counterfactual $A \Rightarrow B$ as $[A](A \rightarrow B)$. The logical systems characterised by semantics of this sort are relevant counterfactual logics. The defeasible nature of the conditional comes from the use of the restricted modal accessibility relations and its relevant character comes from the employment of the ternary relation.

In order to give a concise satisfaction condition for the counterfactual, I define the *relational product* of these two relations. This relational product is $M_A \times R$. $(M_A \times R)stu$ if and only if there is some situation v such that $M_A sv$ and $Rvtu$. $M_A \times R$ is a ternary relation. I abbreviate '$M_A \times R$' by 'R_A'. Relational products very much like this one are used again in Section 5. A concise satisfaction condition for the counterfactual conditional is

$$s \vDash A \Rightarrow B \text{ if and only if for all situations } t, u,$$

$$R_A stu \text{ and } t \vDash A \text{ only if } u \vDash B.$$

I return to defeasible reasoning, accessibility relations, and relational products in Section 5.

3.14 Formal Semantics for Relevant Logic

The semantics that I am putting forward characterises a *relevant logic*. It is controversial as to how to define a relevant logic (see, e.g., [5]), but one necessary condition of a relevant logic is that it has the variable sharing condition; that is, if $A \rightarrow B$ is provable in the logic, then A and B have at least one propositional variable in common [4]. Another requirement of relevant logics is that they do not contain as theorems any schemes that are the so-called paradoxes of implication or entailment, such as

$$(A \wedge \neg A) \rightarrow B, \ B \rightarrow (A \rightarrow A), \ A \rightarrow (B \rightarrow A),$$

and so on.

In order to see exactly how the ternary relation semantics does characterise a relevant logic, I need to make the elements of the formal semantics explicit. A Routley-Meyer frame is a structure $\langle S, 0, R, \bot \rangle$, where S is a non-empty set (the set of situations), 0 is a subset of S (the 'logical' situations), R is a ternary relation on S, and $\bot$ (the incompatibility relation discussed in §3.8) is a binary relation on S, and the following definition and conditions hold:

(Definition of $\leq$) $t \leq u$ if and only if there is a situation s in 0 and $Rstu$

Semantic Conditions on Frames

1. $\leq$ is reflexive, transitive, and antisymmetric;
2. If $s \leq s'$ and $Rs'tu$, then $Rstu$;
3. $\bot$ is symmetrical, i.e. if $s \bot t$ then $t \bot s$;
4. If $s \leq s'$ and $s \bot t$, then $s' \bot t$;
5. For each $s \in S$, there is a $s^* \in S$ such that s is compatible with s^* and if t is compatible with s then $t \leq s^*$;
6. $s = s^{**}$;
7. If $s \leq t$ then $t^* \leq s^*$.

A Routley-Meyer model is a structure $\langle \mathfrak{F}, v \rangle$, where $\mathfrak{F}$ is a Routley-Meyer frame and v is a function from propositional variables to sets of situations that are closed upwards under $\leq$. This means that if $s \leq t$ and s is in $v(p)$, then t is also in $v(p)$. The function v determines a relation $\vDash$ between situations and formulae defined by the following recursive clauses:

- $s \vDash p$ if and only if $s \in v(p)$;
- $s \vDash A \wedge B$ if and only if $s \vDash A$ and $s \vDash B$;
- $s \vDash A \vee B$ if and only if $s \vDash A$ or $s \vDash B$;
- $s \vDash \neg A$ if and only if for all $t \in S$, if $t \vDash A$ then $s \bot t$;
- $s \vDash A \rightarrow B$ if and only if for all $t, u \in S$, if $Rstu$ and $t \vDash A$ then $u \vDash B$.

A formula A is valid on a model if and only if $0 \subseteq [\![A]\!]$, where $[\![A]\!]$ is the set of situations s such that $s \vDash A$. A formula is valid on a class of frames if and only if it is valid on every frame in that class.

The situations in 0 are called 'normal situations'. They contain all the valid formulas (and, by the soundness theorem, all the theorems of the logic). Note that they may not contain as information the fact that each of these theorems is a theorem. For example, $((A \rightarrow B) \wedge (A \rightarrow C)) \rightarrow (A \rightarrow (B \wedge C))$ is in every situation in 0, but there may be situations in 0 that do not contain the information that it is a theorem (or even that it is valid in the frame). The way in which a statement that is an instance of a scheme like this is made information in a particular situation in 0 is not specified by the formal semantics. It could be that there is a proof of the formula available in that situation (see Section 4) or that the situation contains information about the frame as a whole, but the information that a particular instance of this scheme holds could arise by much humbler means. In Section 5, I discuss reasoning largely from the standpoint of normal situations, and take for granted there that agents (at least in some ideal sense) have logical truths available to them when reasoning.

To satisfy Dretske's Xerox principle (§2.8) in the form, $((A \rightarrow B) \wedge (B \rightarrow C)) \rightarrow (A \rightarrow C)$, I also add the following condition:[11]

(CS) If $Rstu$ then there is a situation x such that $Rstx$ and $Rsxu$.

I am not sure how to give an adequate interpretation of this condition in information-theoretic terms, but it would be very good to have one.

The situations in 0 are ones in which the mathematical structure of the frame as a whole is available as information to the agent. I discuss how mathematical facts like those can be information in Section 4.

Facts 2–5 are all provable. Proofs for them can be easily found in the literature (see, e.g., [76, 77, 3]).

Fact 2 (Hereditariness). *For all $s, t \in S$ and all formulae A, if $s \leq t$ and $s \vDash A$, then $t \vDash A$.*

Fact 3 (Semantic Entailment). *For all formulas A, B, $A \rightarrow B$ is valid on a model if and only if for all $s \in S$, if $s \vDash A$ then $s \vDash B$.*

Fact 4 (Routley Star). *For all $s \in S$ and all formulae A, $s \vDash \neg A$ if and only if $s^* \nvDash A$.*

---

[11] 'CS' stands for 'conjunctive syllogism'.

Fact 5 (Contraposition). *For all formulae A and B, if A → B is valid on a model, then ¬B → ¬A is also valid on that model.*

Adding the Modal Operator and Counterfactual Implication

The modal operator S is characterised by a binary relation M_S, which is defined in the semantics:

$M_S st$ if and only if $Rsst$ and $s \leq t$.

In order to treat the defeasible conditional ⇒, for each formula A, I add a modal accessibility relation M_A to the model. The satisfaction condition for restricted modal formulae is

$s \vDash [A]B$ if and only if for all $t \in S$, if $M_A st$, $t \vDash B$,

and $A \Rightarrow B$ is defined as $[A](A \to B)$. The one condition that I add for all the modal accessibility relations is that if $M_A st$ and $s' \leq s$, then $M_A s't$. This allows the proof of Fact 2 for the language with these modal operators.

3.15 Formalising Channel Theory

On the theory of information constructed by Claude Shannon and Warren Weaver [85], communication takes place when information is transferred from a source to a receiver along a *channel*. A channel is also sometimes called a *medium*. The channel, for example, that carries email and social media transmissions is the physical infrastructure of the internet. Channel theory is of particular interest here because it has been formulated using situation theory and the ternary relation semantics.

Channel theory (as a semantics for formal logic) was first constructed by Barwise and Seligman [7, 83, 10], and has been developed further by Greg Restall [74] and Andrew Tedder [87].

The indices in the semantics are called 'sites' and the links between sites are channels. I write

$t \xrightarrow{s} u$

to indicate that s is a channel between t and u. In the theory that I discuss here all sites and channels are situations. When a channel s links the information that A with the information that B, then we write $s \vDash A \to B$ and if, moreover, $t \vDash A$ and $t \xrightarrow{s} u$, then $u \vDash B$.

A channel s might carry the information that $t \vDash A$ carries the information that $u \vDash B$. But there in a channel model there is a manner in which the model itself determines that $t \vDash A$ carries the information that $u \vDash B$. This should not be a strange idea to us by now. In this section I have been discussing models that contain a persistence relation, $\leq$, on situations. The hereditariness fact given in Section 3.14, says that if $s \leq t$ and $s \vDash A$, then $s \vDash A$. The persistence relation is a channel of a sort – the model as a whole transmits information along that relation.

Barwise [7] sets out four conditions on channel theoretic models (see also [60]). I examine only the first two here:

1. (Xerox) The model should satisfy the Xerox principle;
2. (Entailment as Information Flow) If A entails B (in the sense of Section Fact 3 above) then in the model $s \vDash A$ carries the information that $s \vDash B$;

I begin my explanation of these conditions by explaining the notion of entailment in a model.

The primary notion of semantic entailment in possible worlds semantics and other indexed model theories is that of informational closure – that is, in a model A entails B if and only if in every index that satisfies A also satisfies B. If we use this as a definition in a channel model that the idea that entailment is information flow becomes merely definitional. But there is another way of thinking about entailment. There is a special index (or set of indices) at which the entailments of the model are all satisfied. This is the way in which entailments (and logical truth more generally) are understood in the semantics for relevant logic (see §3.14). According to Fact 3, if an implication, $A \rightarrow B$ is true in every situation in 0, then for every situation s, if $s \vDash A$ then $s \vDash B$.

Barwise [7] and Restall [74] show how to represent channel theory in the Routley-Meyer semantics.[12] This is yet another way in which information theory has been used to help logic – the information theoretic reading gives a philosophically useful way to understand the ternary relation semantics. On this reading, $Rstu$ is understood as saying that s is a channel between t and u. If $s \in 0$, then $t \leq u$ and for every situation t there is some $s \in 0$ such that $Rstt$ – this s is the identity of t.

3.16 The Logic

The base logic is the relevant logic **DJ**. Disjunction is defined as follows:

$$A \vee B =_{df} \neg(\neg A \wedge \neg B)$$

Here is an axiomatisation of **DJ**.

---

[12] [87] shows that even the models for quite weak relevant are closed under the postulates needed for channel theory, such as composition of channels.

Axiom Schemata	**Rules**

1. $A \rightarrow A$

2. $((A \rightarrow B) \wedge (B \rightarrow C)) \rightarrow (A \rightarrow C)$

3. $((A \rightarrow C) \wedge (B \rightarrow C)) \rightarrow ((A \vee B) \rightarrow C)$

$$\frac{\vdash A \rightarrow B \quad \vdash A}{\vdash B}$$

4. $(A \wedge B) \rightarrow (B \wedge A)$

5. $(A \rightarrow C) \rightarrow ((A \wedge B) \rightarrow C)$

$$\frac{\vdash A \rightarrow B \quad \vdash C \rightarrow D}{\vdash (B \rightarrow C) \rightarrow (A \rightarrow D)}$$

6. $((A \rightarrow B) \wedge (A \rightarrow C)) \rightarrow (A \rightarrow (B \wedge C))$

7. $(A \wedge (B \vee C)) \rightarrow ((A \wedge B) \vee (A \wedge C))$

$$\frac{\vdash A \rightarrow \neg B}{\vdash B \rightarrow \neg A}$$

8. $\neg\neg A \rightarrow A$

To the language, I add the modal operators E, S, and for each formula A, the operator $[A]$. To the logic, I add the axiom schema, $(OA \wedge OB) \rightarrow O(A \wedge B)$ and the rule, $\vdash A \rightarrow B$ implies $\vdash OA \rightarrow OB$, where O can be uniformly replaced with either E, S, or $[A]$. For E and S, there are further axioms: $((A \rightarrow B) \wedge EA) \rightarrow EB$, $EA \rightarrow SA$, $((A \rightarrow B) \wedge SA) \rightarrow SB$, and $A \rightarrow SA$.

4 Information, Identity, and Logical Truths

4.1 Introduction

On the possible world semantics for standard modal logics, a statement is logically true if and only if it is true in every possible world (in every model). On the CBH theory (§3.3), a statement that is true in every possible world carries no semantic information at all. But we learn logical truths, we wonder about whether statements are logically true, and so on. It seems that there is information captured by logical truths. The relevant logic approach is somewhat better. Not all logical truths are true in all situations. But there is still a related problem with that semantics of information. On a model, $\mathfrak{M}$, $A \vDash_{\mathfrak{M}} B$, if and only if $[\![A]\!] \subseteq [\![B]\!]$; that is, A includes the information that B. Intuitively, however, in many cases we can have access to the information that A without having access to the information that B even when A entails B. Both of these problems – that logical truths carry no information and that deductions from premises yield no extra information – have been called by Jaakko Hintikka the 'scandal of deduction' [41].[13]

I offer two ways out of these puzzles. The first is to treat them as a problem about the *extraction of information*. As I say in Section 2.4, I distinguish between implicit and explicit information. If $A \vDash_{\mathfrak{M}} B$, then the model $\mathfrak{M}$ says that one who is in possession of the information that A is in possession of the information that B, but this latter information is often merely implicit. To make

---

[13] For a very detailed explanation and analysis of Hintikka's own view of information, see [84].

it explicit it has to be extracted somehow. This process of extraction can be evaluated in terms of a reasonable conception of the quantity of information. This quantity is a measure of how hard it is to extract the information, that is, to make it explicit. The second way out of the puzzle is to treat the quantity of information in *agent-relative terms*; that is, to look at how much work it would be to incorporate a proposition into one's set of beliefs, preferences, and emotional attitudes.

In making this move away from worlds or situation semantics to measures of the difficulty of extraction, I am changing approaches to information from information as range to information as code (see §2.1). Consider again the example of $(p \supset q) \vee (q \supset r)$. In classical logic, this statement is equivalent to every other logical truth. For example it is equivalent to $p \vee \neg p$. What is different about they is that considered as sentences, or as the structured propositions that they express, they have different internal structures. Extracting the fact that a particular sentence of structured proposition represents the one logically true unstructured proposition (i.e. the set of possible worlds itself) will be easy or difficult depending on the sentence or structured proposition.

Similar problems, and solutions, appear in other aspects of informational semantics. In Frege's puzzle about informative identity statements, the problem arises when we have two expressions (such as names) that have the same semantic content. The informational distinction between two statements that in fact express identities holding between the same entities consists in differences between the ways in which we extract the information that the identities hold. In order to use the information as coding approach to Frege's puzzle we need to have a way of representing explicit information that makes a distinction between the structured propositions concerned. It is this topic to which I first turn.

4.2 Frege's Puzzle

Frege's famous puzzle about proper names was couched in terms of 'cognitive value' [33], but it loses nothing by placing it in the context of the theory of semantic information. The two proper names 'Hesperus' and 'Phosphorus' refer to the same thing; that is, they both refer to the planet Venus. If, as the direct reference theory holds, proper names are mere labels for things, then the proposition expressed by the sentence

    (i) Hesperus is identical to Hesperus

is the same as the proposition expressed by

    (ii) Phosphorus is identical to Hesperus.

Sentence (ii), however, seems to be informative in a way that (i) is not.

Frege's reaction to the puzzle is to reject Mill's theory of proper names and instead claim that each proper name has a unique meaning or sense. Frege says that the sense of a name is a 'mode of presentation' [33]. Leonard Linsky interprets a modes of presentation, moreover, as a 'criterion for the identification for the object denoted by the name' [51, p 10]. Most Frege interpreters now seem to take these criteria to be definite descriptions, and most of the examples in 'On Sense and Reference' are definite descriptions. Whether Frege really thinks that all modes of presentation can be represented by definite descriptions, however, is not clear. At any rate, the thesis that different names have different senses does solve the problem by allowing us to understand an identity statement as making a claim about a relation between two senses, that it, that they have the same referent. Thus, (i) says that the sense of 'Hesperus' has the same referent as itself and (ii) tells us that the senses of 'Hesperus' and 'Phosphorus' have the same referent.

Frege's view has obvious connections with the theory of semantic information. An identity statement, on this view, is about the connection between two ways of identifying an object. When one says, 'the Morning Star is identical to the Evening Star', one is saying that a single thing can be identified in one way just before sunrise and in another way just after sunset. Thus there is information in the statement both about an entity (Venus) and about our ways of locating that entity.

Frege's solution, however, presupposes that proper names have cognitive value. Mill's theory, and its successor, the theory of direct reference, holds that names are mere labels and do not refer to things by means of a sense or any other mediating entity. I do not want to adjudicate between these theories of reference here. This is not a book about the philosophy of language, but rather I indicate some alternative devices for distinguishing informative from non-informative identity statements.

4.3 Content Again

The question that we need to answer now is how to reply to Frege's puzzle in the framework of the theory of structured propositions. At first glance, it seems as though one should represent the content of 'Hesperus is Phosphorus', 'Hesperus is Hesperus', and 'Phosphorus is Venus' all by the structured proposition $\langle =, e, e \rangle$, where e is Venus. But, in terms of information content, this seems wrong. The problem is that the shape of the words used to refer to Venus seem to matter, but the words are not included in the structured proposition.

One reply to this problem is provided by the causal-descriptive theory of meaning developed by Fred Kroon [49]. On the causal-descriptivist theory, names are not just labels (as they are on the direct reference theory) but rather carry a minimal amount of content. The content of a name **n** on an occasion in which I use it that can be represented perspicuously by the phrase 'the object that caused my use of the name **n**'. Although this theory is clearly indebted to Kripke's causal theory of names, it also agrees with Frege's view that identity sentences provide information about entities and about ways of locating those entities.

So, 'Hesperus is Phosphorus', as I say it, can be translated perspicuously into first-order logic as

$\exists x \exists y ($Caused my use of 'Hesperus'$(x) \wedge$

Caused my use of 'Phosphorus'$(y) \wedge x = y)$

Note that in these translations the phrases must be given wide scope that are used to express the fact that the name used is caused by an object that is then predicated of in some manner. In translating 'Hesperus is necessarily Phosphorus' we want

$\exists x \exists y ($Caused my use of 'Hesperus'$(x) \wedge$

Caused my use of 'Phosphorus'$(y) \wedge \Box x = y)$,

not

$\Box \exists x \exists y ($Caused my use of 'Hesperus'$(x) \wedge$

Caused my use of 'Phosphorus'$(y) \wedge x = y)$.

This latter sentence is clearly false. It could have been that the objects that caused my uses of 'Hesperus' and 'Phosphorus' were distinct from one another. But all of these sentences can be represented unproblematically in the theory of structured propositions.

Adopting this sort of solution for statements that contain names, however, is not enough. The same problem carries over to other sorts of referring expressions for which direct reference have been given. Consider, for example, demonstrative pronouns. 'This' and 'that', used demonstratively, seem like pure labels and seem to have no descriptive content. Here is a Frege-like example concerning demonstratives. Suppose that one has two means of perceptual access to an object. Let's say that one of the images that one sees is a reflection but the agent does not realise this. They say 'This is much bigger than that' pointing at two images of the same thing. It seems then that we need, on the causal descriptivist theory applied to demonstrative pronouns, to say that this sentence is to be read as saying that the object x to which I have demonstrated and used 'this' and the object y to which I have demonstrated and used 'that' are such that x is much bigger than y. Thus it seems that the technique that the causal-descriptivist theory uses to deal with names can be extended to treat other apparently directly referring expression.[14]

4.4 Extracting Logical Truths

On possible world semantics, logical truths are true in all possible worlds. They all represent the same unstructured proposition, that is, W itself. On the semantics for relevant logic, logical truths may express different unstructured propositions, all of which overlap with the set 0. But, formulae that look very different may turn out, even in relevant logic, to be logically equivalent to one another, and hence express the same proposition.[15]

The problem of the information content of logical equivalences is really another form of Frege's puzzle. Frege's puzzle is about distinct linguistic expressions referring to the same individual. The problem of logical equivalences is about distinct linguistic expressions expressing the same entity (a set of worlds or situations). This similarity of problems suggests that their answers may be similar in nature.

The first element of the answer to the problems of the information content of logical truths and of logical equivalences does appeal to structured propositions. A logical truth, say, $p \rightarrow p$, expresses a structured proposition – in this case, $\langle \rightarrow, \langle \mathbf{p}, \mathbf{p} \rangle \rangle$, where boldface '$p$' is the structured proposition expressed by p.

The appeal to structured propositions, however, is only part of the solution to these problems. The information that is in question here is not just about the structured proposition. It is about the relationship between the structured proposition and another structured proposition (in the problem of logical equivalences) or the relationship between the structured proposition and a model or class of models (in the problem of logical truths).

In order to proceed, I distinguish between two senses of having the information that some proposition is a logical truth. One sense is of having the information that a proposition A is logically true simpliciter. This is distinguished

---

[14] Another approach to Frege's puzzle is to use two-dimensional semantics. To construct a two-dimensional semantics, we need to add a set of *contexts of utterance* to our model. These can be situations in the sense of Section 3. A proper name gets its reference from the context in which it uttered. A two-dimensional proposition is a function from contexts of utterance to sets of indices. The 2D proposition *Hesperus is Phosphorus* is different from *Hesperus is Hesperus* because there are contexts of utterance in which 'Hesperus' and 'Phosphorus' denote the same thing.

[15] In very weak relevant logics, most of the equivalences one can prove seem rather trivial and in some of these logics equivalent formulae even have fairly similar syntactic structure [52].

from the second sense of having the information that A is a logical truth in some logical system or other (i.e. a theorem of that system or true in some particular class of models). The latter is simpler, so I start with that.

There are many ways of gaining information about logical systems, both proof-theoretic and model-theoretic. Here I use the example of someone's setting down a Hilbert-style axiom system – a list of axioms or axiom schemata and a list of rules under which the set of theorems is closed. The axioms of a system hold by stipulation. In fact, the axioms and rules of the system define the system in question. The stipulation of these axioms makes them true of the system, and hence this stipulation is an information producing process (it is one of the sorts of conventions referred to by Barwise and Selgiman – see §2.7). So is the process of proving theorems in the logic by the means proscribed by the stipulation of the system.

Let us examine this a bit more closely. Suppose that in a situation s someone defines a logic L such that it contains the following rule of modus ponens:

$$\frac{\vdash_L A \supset B \quad \vdash_L A}{\vdash_L B}$$

(where '$\vdash_L$' means 'is a theorem of L'). In the local logic of the agent in s, the following implication holds:

$$(\vdash_L A \supset B \wedge \vdash_L A) \rightarrow \vdash_L B$$

If the agent then proves $\vdash_L A$ and $\vdash_L A \supset B$ these become explicit in her information state and $\vdash_L B$ becomes at least implicit in that state. If she applies modus ponens to those explicitly held propositions, then $\vdash_L B$ becomes explicit in her state. The process is a valid means of producing the theorems of L regardless of whether those theorems are really valid or not.

The question of the informational status of the real logic of the model itself is much more difficult. In the possible worlds models of information, if A is a logical truth then the information that A is true is in all worlds. In the models for relevant logic, if A is logically true then the information that it is true is in all situations in the set 0. My explanation of what 0 is in Section 3.14 is quite hand-wavy. I merely say that it is the set of situations that contain accurate information about the model as a whole. It is now the incumbent on me to explain this idea more fully.

In line with the theory of information that I outline in Section 2, in order for there to be information about logical truths simpliciter, these truths all need to seem to be grounded in truthmakers. So the question arises, what are the truthmakers for logical truths and how is the way in which we discover logical truths related to those truthmakers. Some philosophers claim that there are processes of a priori justification that determine what the logical truths are. These views, however, have been thrown into question by the emergence of alternative logical systems, like those that are discussed in Section 3. With the rise of alternative logical systems, epistemologies of logic have developed according to which individuals must argue for the logic that they wish to adopt on abductive grounds or through the use of reflective equilibrium [80, 92, 70]. If logical truths reflect some platonic reality, then it is hard to see how the relationship between this reality and abduction or reflective equilibrium could be considered even a fairly reliable way to access these truths. Such processes might be adequate for knowledge about logic (this depends on the nature of the justification needed for knowledge) but it would seem not to be adequate for information.

There are, however, philosophies of logic that postulate more accessible truthmakers for logical truths. Stephen Read [72], for example, claims that the truthmakers for logical truths are proofs. Thus, one who is possession of a proof has the information that what is proven is a logical truth. Penelopy Maddy [53] holds that the true logic, which she calls 'rudimentary logic' reflects the very basic structure of the universe.[16] An awareness of this structure, perhaps a tacit awareness, may be enough to say that the principles of this logic are possessed as information. Similarly, Gillian Russell [80] thinks that the laws of logic reflect our use of language. Philosophical argument concerning whether a given principle is in fact a law may require explicit reflection on our use of language, but the ability to use language may itself be enough to give an individual logical information. Here there is a parallel with simple perceptual information. Consider a case in which someone sees a dog. Seeing the dog is enough for the person to have the information that there is a dog in a particular location. One does not have to reflect on the fact that they see the dog in order to possess such information. Similarly the ability to use language correctly may be enough for an agent to possess logical knowledge.

The best route to a theory of logical information seems right now to adopt a view that allows agents to have access to the truthmakers for logical truths. To bring the discussion back to the situations in the set 0 of a relevant logic model, these are the situations in which these truthmakers are in fact accessible to the agent.

---

[16] Maddy [53, ch III.7] explicitly denies that relevant logic is a good way of representing the structure of the universe or cognition and so her view might not provide a good basis for my own epistemology of logic.

4.5 Upstream and Downstream

In Section 4.4, I suggest statements such as '*A* is a theorem of the logic *L*' and '*A* is a logical truth' can have real informational content. On the CBH theory, however, logical truths do not have any positive information. It assigns to every logical truth the quantity zero as the quantity of information that it has. This is an extremely counter-intuitive view. When we are informed that a formula that we have never considered before is in fact a theorem, it seems that we learn something. Qualitatively, what we learn is the sort of information described in Section 4.4. In this section, I discuss a theory that assigns non-trivial quantities to the information contained in theorems and in propositions about the theorems of logical systems. Once again, the latter topic is easier so I begin with that.

In order to approach this topic, let's think a bit more about what it means to be informed. Certain salient aspects of processes of being informed are *upstream*. The acts involved in extracting the information, and their difficulty, are all upstream – they occur before the agent can be said to have been informed. In order to measure these upstream difficulties concerning *A* being a theorem of *L* one might use a measure of the complexity of proving that *A* in *L*. There are also *downstream* effects of being informed. When I first heard that Trump had been elected, I had to revise many of my beliefs about the sanity of the public, the future of democracy, and so on, and I changed some important emotional attitudes. Measuring the difficulties involved in making these changes gives us another notion of the quantity of information of that proposition.

Measures of upstream difficulties are provided by the mathematical field of *complexity theory*. There are various ways of measuring the complexity of logical proofs, but one that is particularly dominant is a measure of the length (in steps) of the shortest proof of a formula (see, e.g., [19, 47]). One problem with measures like this is that there are different proof systems and in these different systems the same theorem can have a long or a very short proof. Thus, the quantity of information in a statement of the form '*A* is a theorem of *L*' should be understood relative to a proof system.

Another issue is that the length of a proof, however, for people is not always a good measure of its difficultly. Consider the following example that I give to upper-level undergraduates. The following is a fairly standard axiomatisation of the pure implicational fragment of Intuitionist Logic. Its rules are modus ponens and a rule of uniform substitution for propositional variables. It has two axioms:

1. $p \supset (q \supset p)$
2. $(p \supset (q \supset r)) \supset ((p \supset q) \supset (p \supset r))$

The students are given these axioms and rules then asked to prove $p \supset p$. The vast majority of them find this question extremely hard and give up. But there is a short proof:

1. $p \supset (q \supset p)$ axiom 1
2. $(p \supset (q \supset p)) \supset ((p \supset q) \supset (p \supset p))$ axiom 2, Uniform Substitution r/p
3. $(p \supset q) \supset (p \supset p)$ 1, 2, modus ponens
4. $(p \supset (q \supset p)) \supset (p \supset p)$ 3, Uniform Substitution $q/q \supset p$
5. $p \supset p$ 1, 4, modus ponens

The trick is the creative use of the uniform substitution rule at lines 2 and 4. This need for creativity is not incorporated into the sort of measures that complexity theory employs, but even if there is a need for more refinement of the measures of the difficulty of proving theorems, we can often equate the information contained in the statement 'A is a theorem of L' with the difficulty of proving L.

Dan Sperber and Deirdre Wilson's relevance theory [86] employs a concept of the downstream effects of pieces of information. On their view, a statement in a conversation is relevant to a participant in that conversation if accepting it will cause positive cognitive effects (in particular, changes or additions to his beliefs). On their view, we attempt to maximise the relevance of statements made in a conversation; that is, one infers what the speaker has in mind based largely on the 'presumption' that the speaker is trying to convey something that is relevant to the hearer. Although Sperber and Wilson often talk about maximising relevance, optimal relevance, and when a statement has enough relevance, they do not provide an explicit numerical measure of relevance. This is not a flaw in their theory – they may not need such a measure. But perhaps one could be constructed that satisfies their constraints on what counts as more or less relevance.

The point here is not that we need a specific numerical measure of the downstream quantity of information, but rather that logical truths and facts about what is derivable in a system can have rather a lot of relevance. The existence of the theory of proof complexity and relevance theory show that it is coherent to claim that, from both upstream and downstream perspectives, we can assign to logical truths and truths about what propositions are theorems of logical systems positive quantities of information. That these notions may need further refinement to be exact or to apply to the human understanding of the difficulty of proof do not show that such measures are impossible, but rather that more work needs to be done.

5 Updating Information

5.1 Introduction

The question that I discuss in this section is how one is to update his or her information state when new information comes to light. A classical logic of updates
has been constructed in the framework of dynamic logic (see §5.2). There has
been relatively little work done to construct non-classical dynamic logics, but
some has been undertaken, especially by Marta Bilková, Vít Punčochář, Igor
Sedlár, and Andrew Tedder (see [88, 62] for additional references). What I say
in this section is quite sketchy and very tentative.

   If we were to follow the theorists who claim that all information is true, then
the updating of information states should be easily described. All integration
of information would be is, in effect, the addition of new information. No old
information would need to be deleted. If, however, we do what I have been
doing in this Element and take some information to be false, then things are
not so easy. Sometimes new information undermines the reasons for accepting
other propositions as information. This sort of undermining needs to be discussed. The processes of informational updating follows the informal outline
of defeasible logic described in Section 3.

5.2 Dynamic Logic

In order to formalise updating within the logic itself, I follow Alexandru Baltag,
Sonja Smets, Johan van Benthem, and others [6, 90] in treating informational
updates and revisions in a sort of *dynamic logic*. Dynamic logic was originally
developed by Vaughan Pratt [68] as a logic in which computer programs can be
represented. This section is a very brief introduction to dynamic logic. I follow
Robert Goldblatt [39, ch 10] in my presentation of dynamic logic.

   The semantics for dynamic logic has a lot in common with the semantics for
defeasible conditionals given in Section 3.13. The semantics for dynamic logic
uses binary accessibility relations on the indices of the model. These indices
can be understood as possible states of a computer. For dynamic logic, like
the logic of defeasible conditionals, each accessibility relation has a subscript.
Unlike conditional logic, these subscripts are not formulae, but *programs*. A
program is thought of as an action that links one index to another or to one of a
set of indices. For example, where A is a formula, the program $?A$ says to test
whether A is true in the present situation. If it fails to be true, $?A$ says then to
stop.

   The language contains a set of primitive programs and program operators
that allow one to form complex programs. For example, if α and β are programs, then $\alpha;\beta$ is the programs that says first to perform α and then to

perform β. Where M_α is the accessibility relation associated with α and M_β is the accessibility relation associated with β,

$M_{\alpha;\beta}st$ if and only if there is an index u, $M_\alpha su$ and $M_\beta ut$.

The accessibility relation for $\alpha;\beta$ is the relational product of the accessibility relations for α and β (see §3.13). The accessibility relation for the a test program, $?A$, is

$M_{?A}st$ if and only if both $s = t$ and $t \vDash A$.

If $s \nvDash A$, then s is not related to anything by $M_{?A}$.[17] The understanding of a failed or aborted program in this semantics is to treat indices where the program has aborted as related to no other indices ('dead ends').

Each program α determines a necessity operator, $[\alpha]$. The satisfaction clause for $[\alpha]$ is

$s \vDash [\alpha]A$ if and only if for all $t \in S$, if $M_\alpha st$, then $t \vDash A$.

The formula '$[\alpha]A$' is read as saying 'after the performance of α, A'.

Translating the semantics of dynamic logic into the Routley-Meyer framework is quite tricky. Consider for example, **abort**. The accessibility relation M_{abort} is the empty relation; it does not relate indices to anything. In dynamic logic based on classical logic, we can represent this relation by the axiom $[\text{abort}]A$, which says that after **abort** is performed, everything is true, since there is no 'after **abort**'. If we satisfy $[\text{abort}]A$ at every index in a Routley-Meyer model, however, we make valid

$B \rightarrow [\text{abort}]A$,

which, from a relevant point of view, is repugnant. Sedlár, Punčochář, and Tedder [71] argue that a relevant semantics for dynamic logic does not need to have an **abort** program, and omitting it may be the best solution to this difficulty.

5.3 Public Announcement Logic

One sort of action that has been of particular importance in the information theory literature is the public announcement. When a trustworthy public announcement is made, people often have reason to update their information

---

[17] As I say in Section 3.13, to set out this sort of semantics formally, it is best to add a set of propositions to the definition of a frame, but doing this for each new language in this Element would be rather onerous and would add little to the understanding of the various logical systems.

Figure 2 Logicians ordering beer

states. As an example I use a joke that is a very simple variant on Rohit Parikh's [67] muddy children example. The joke is known as the beery logicians, and here it is in cartoon form (Figure 2).[18]

Let's consider the changing information states of the logician in the striped shirt. She knows that the others will answer 'no' if they do not want a beer, but not having access to the inner states of the others, cannot say for sure if the others do or do not want a beer. When each of the other two logicians answers 'I do not know', the last logician has the information that the others want a beer and so updates her own conscious information state accordingly.

The process begins with the question, 'does everyone want a beer?' For each of the logicians, there are eight possibilities; that is, the worlds in their information states are partitioned into eight classes that we can label, WWW, WWD, WDD, WDW, DWW, DWD, DDW, DDD (where W = Wants Beer and D = Doesn't Want Beer). Only WWW corresponds to a 'yes' answer to the original question the others all correspond to 'no'.

[18] This is Spiked Math comic number 445 and is licensed under a Creative Commons License (Non-Commercial ShareAlike 3.0 Unported License).

At the start, the stripy logician has the information that she wants a beer. Thus, her state contains the information

$WWW \lor DWW \lor WDW \lor DDW.$

When the first logician answers, 'I don't know' to the question, the stripy logician knows that the first logician is rejecting both DWW and DDW (see §5.6). The stripy logician takes the first logician's denial to be accurate, and so updates to

$WWW \lor WDW.$

When the second logician says, 'I don't know', the stripy logician takes this as a denial that WDW, and so updates to

$WWW,$

and so says 'yes'.

In order to formalise reasoning about public announcements, van Benthem has formulated a public announcement logic (PAL). In order to construct PAL, for each formula, the operator $[!A]$ is added to the language. The statement '$[!A]B$' means, 'after the announcement that A, B'. In the dynamic logical semantics, $!A$ is treated as a program.

In the next section, I make some remarks aiming towards the creation of a semantics for a relevant version of PAL.

5.4 Non-Defeasible Updating

Perhaps the best way of modelling the reasoning involved in the Beery Logicians puzzle is to treat the informational updates as *non-defeasible*. I take $M_{!A}$ to update contexts of reception. This means that after an announcement, an agent is in a different situation. Announcements change situations – they add information. Thus,

(ND) $M_{!A}st$ only if $s \leq t$.

This non-defeasibility postulate makes valid the following schema:

$B \rightarrow [!A]B$

The way in which A is incorporated into updates of situations by A is more interesting and needs some motivation.

In Section 5.3, I only discuss updating from the perspective of normal situations. Thinking of non-normal situations as completely different from normal situations, however, makes me rather uncomfortable. The meanings of connectives should be given by their satisfaction conditions and, if a connective like

[! *A*] means the same thing in a non-normal situation as in a normal situation it should have the same satisfaction condition. The problem is that if we under-stand [! *A*] as telling us what happens when we update a situation by *A*, then it seems hard to understand how that update can fail to contain the information that *A*.

In Section 3, situations are introduced as being (potential) parts of a world. If we understand updates as telling us about what happens in the world, rather than in one's present situation, then things get a bit clearer. Recall that on the situated inference theory (explained in §3.12), the ternary relation of the Routley-Meyer semantics is to be understood as telling us about what an agent can infer about situations in their present world. The set of situations Rst determines what the agent can infer about on the basis of the information in s and the hypothesis of t. Such inferences can be represented by conditionals of the form 'from the perspective of s, if t holds in the same world as s, then ...'.

Now, let's read [! *A*]*B* as saying that after the announcement that *A*, *B* holds (somewhere in this world). Let R_A be a binary relation between situations such that $R_A st$ if and only if there is some situation u such that $u \vDash A$ and $Rsut$. Then $s \vDash A \rightarrow B$ if and only if for all t for which $R_A st$, $t \vDash B$. It would seem natural, then, to have $M_{!A}s \subseteq R_A s$. If we do this, then we make valid the following schema:[19]

$$(A \rightarrow B) \rightarrow [!\,A]B$$

We also get a lot of what we want out of a logic of announcements. For example, we make valid the schema,

Success : [! *A*]*A*,

because for all normal situations, $R_A s$ is a subset of $[\![A]\!]$. The usual modal aggregation principle is valid:

Aggregation : $([!\,A]B \wedge [!\,A]C) \rightarrow [!\,A](B \wedge C)$.

In addition, the 'regularity' rule

$$\frac{\vdash B \rightarrow C}{\vdash [!\,A]B \rightarrow [!\,A]C}$$

is valid.

---

[19] We also need to add the condition that if $s \leq t$, then $M_{!A}t \subseteq M_{!A}s$.

5.5 Information, Hard and Soft

When one gains new information, his or her context of reception changes. I just saw that a construction company van is parked in front of my neighbours' house. I now change the way that I was thinking about my day. I had expected a nice quiet day that would make writing easier. I have now updated my situation in the sense that my expectations have changed as has my information about my expectations. And if I hear some sawing or banging noises from next door, I will be able to place them into an informational framework that one might call *the neighbours are getting work done on their house*. My context of reception has now changed to include both the new information about the van and my new expectations.

I add another modality, $[*A]$, for each formula A. I use an asterisk to mark a revision to allude to revision operator in the logic of belief revision. As in Section 5.4, I set $M_{*A}s \subseteq R_A s$. M_{*A} says what sorts of situations one ends up in after updates to include A (somewhere in the world). This new modality is a generalisation of the modality of PAL, and it is importantly different.

If updating information were always the mere addition of information (which it would be if all information were true), then I would add the condition that if $M_{*+A}st$ then $s \leq t$. But on my view, misinformation is information. In updating information, sometimes old information is relinquished. If the agent in the firefighters case were to see a book, *Terrorist Manual, Volume II: Using Disinformation to Increase Harm*, in the pocket of the supposed firefighter number 1 that would undermine the old informational inference from Person 1's being dressed as a firefighter to Person 1's being a firefighter.

Some information is *harder* than other information in the same way that some evidence used in courts of law is harder than other evidence. The information that person 1 is dressed as a firefighter is harder evidence than that he is a firefighter. The evidence that he has that book in his pocket is also harder evidence than that he is a firefighter.

We can think of the hardness or softness of information in much the same way that researchers in the belief revision tradition think of *epistemic entrenchment* (see [36, 35]). An epistemic entrenchment relation tells us which beliefs are more strongly held by an agent. When relinquishing a belief (perhaps to incorporate a contradicting belief), one must also give up other beliefs so that the remaining propositions no longer imply the old belief. This process often requires choices, and these are supposed to be guided by the entrenchment relation. One is supposed to give up his or her less entrenched beliefs and keep the more entrenched ones.

That new information can undermine old information means that updates can be non-monotonic. We don't want to make valid $[*A]C \rightarrow [*(A \wedge B)]C$. One way of doing this is to follow the ideas set out in Section 3.13. Recall that $A \Rightarrow B$ is in s if and only if for all situations t and u, if $R_A stu$ and $t \vDash A$, then $u \vDash B$. The relation R_A is created from a product of M_A and R and that $M_A st$ if and only if t accords with the background conditions of A relative to s. I do much the same thing here with regard to updates. I set $M_{*A}s \subseteq R_A^A s$, where $R_A^A s$ is the set of situations t such that there is some $u \vDash A$ and $R_A sut$. The idea here is that when a situation s is to be updated by A, first we find a situation that is a modification of s that contains the background conditions related to A (and not those that are undermined by A) and then we update using the ternary relation from the semantics for relevant logics. This gives us a non-monotonic treatment of updating.

The postulate

$$M_{*A}s \subseteq R_A s$$

makes valid the thesis

$$(A \Rightarrow B) \rightarrow [*A]B.$$

In addition, the success postulate ($[*A]A$), the aggregation postulate (($[*A]B \wedge [*A]C) \rightarrow [*A](B \wedge C)$) and the salient version of the regularity rule are valid.

5.6 Negative Information

One might object to the way in which I represent the reasoning in the beery logicians example and claim that I have smuggled uses of *disjunctive syllogism*. Disjunctive syllogism is the following rule of inference:

$$\frac{A \vee B \quad \neg A}{B}$$

When the beery logicians say, 'I don't know', the stripy logician eliminates options from the disjunction of the original eight possibilities, by a process that looks like disjunctive syllogism. Paraconsistent and relevant logicians (for the most part), however, reject disjunctive syllogism. The problem concerns the following argument given by C.I. Lewis [50]:

1.	$A \wedge \neg A$	Premise
2.	A	1, conjunction elimination
3.	$A \vee B$	2, disjunction introduction
4.	$\neg A$	1, conjunction elimination
5.	B	3,4, disjunction syllogism

If we accept disjunctive syllogism and these other rules of inference, then we allow that anything can be inferred from a contradiction. By the deduction theorem, it would seem then that we should accept that contradictory propositions carry all information and the treatment of conflicting information that I give in Section 3 would be made unworkable.

Instead, I treat the logicians' utterances of 'I don't know' as *denials* rather than as assertions of negations. This is a distinction that we need when dealing with various sorts of non-classical logics. An assertion of ¬*A* need not eliminate the possibility that *A*, according to paraconsistent logicians. We need another way to understand the elimination of information, and that is to distinguish between the speech acts of asserting a negation and making a denial. Disjunctive syllogism, in the form *A* ∨ *B* is asserted and *A* is denied, therefore *B* is asserted, is valid in a pragmatic (rather than purely semantic sense) of validity.

The theory of negation I outline in Section 3.8, makes information about negations into a form of *positive* information. If a negation, ¬*A*, is in a situation *s*, then *s* is incompatible with *A*. To say that *A* fails to hold in a situation is rather different. As I write this, I am in my lounge with my dog only. In this situation that consists in the information available to me right now, there is the information that my dog is asleep on our sofa, but there is no information about whereabouts of my partner (other than that she is not in the same room as me and the dog). Let *G* stand 'Sue is in the garden'. Then this situation contains neither *G* nor ¬*G*. If you were to ask me right now whether Sue is in the garden, I would say, 'I don't know'. This utterance, I suggest, is often used to make a denial (i.e. to deny the having of certain sorts of information) rather than an assertion, or, only secondarily to make an assertion about my state of knowledge.

The speech act of denial has a counterpart in the mental act of rejection. It also has an informational counterpart in which a proposition is removed from a situation. Here we could add an operator $[-A]$ that represents the removal of *A*. It would be the counterpart of the contraction operator of the logic of belief revision. We would need to prove that if $s \in 0$ and $M_{-A}st$ only if $t \nvDash A$. The proviso that *s* is in 0 is needed (once again) because otherwise we would make valid $[-A]A \rightarrow B$ for arbitrary formulae *B*.

At the moment, I am not sure how to give a semantics for or axiomatise a dynamic logic of denial and I leave it as an open problem.[20]

---

[20] André Fuhrmann's [34] theory of the contraction of inconsistent theories might provide a good basis for such a theory.

6 Information and Probability

6.1 Introduction

In Section 3.3, I outline the CBH theory of information. The CBH theory places probability measures on propositions as sets of possible worlds. It attributes more information to propositions that are true in fewer worlds and less information to those that are true in more worlds. The set of possible worlds itself (the one logical truth) has zero information. The empty set (the logical falsehood) has maximal information.

In Section 4, I claim that the CBH theory is unhelpful when it comes to thinking about the amount of information contained in logical derivations, logical equivalences, and in logical truths. But what of contingencies? It turns out that CBH is quite intuitive in this regard. For example, right now, I am in my office. I have available to me information about the weather in Wellington. All I have to do is to look out the window and I can see what the weather is. If I see that it is cloudy, this will give me very little information. When I came into the office this morning, it was cloudy and I expected it to stay that way all day. If I turn around and see that the clouds have cleared, then I have more information, because I have learned something new and slightly surprising. If I see a tornado over the harbour, then I have a lot more information, because this is very surprising. It is this notion of the quantity of information that CBH captures well.

CBH has other virtues. In particular it comes with a view of updating information. One can conditionalise on new information and the result is a new probability measure on the set of propositions.

The CBH measure of information is a downstream measure (in the terminology of Section 4). Recall that on Sperber and Wilson downstream notion of information, a proposition contains more information the more that one would have to change their beliefs if they were to accept it. To some extent this idea is incorporated into the CBH theory as well. A surprising proposition is one with low prior probability. If an agent comes to accept a surprising proposition, they will have to change their other probabilities a great deal. Unlike the proof complexity measure, CBH does not rate a proposition as having more information if its truth or falsity is difficult to discover.

In this section, I explore the relationship between probability and information further. I discuss the nature of the probabilities involved in information and the relationship between probability and the different logical systems that I discuss in the earlier sections of this Element.

6.2 Probability Functions

The classical theory of probability is usefully captured by Andrey Kolmorgorov's axioms. His axioms are on a set of points, known as a 'event space'. We can think of Kolmogorov's event space as a set of possible worlds. An event type is a set of events. Here I substitute the notion of a set of possible worlds for Kolmogorov's event space, and treat worlds as events. Later, I substitute situations for events. Propositions as sets of worlds are assessed probabilities. Following are some simplified Kolmogorov axioms for probability, adapted to the theory of possible worlds.

Kolmogorov's Axioms for a Semantic Theory of Probability. Let W be a set of worlds and $Prop$ a set of propositions on W. $Prop$ is closed under intersection, union, and relative complement.

A *probability function* is a function from $Prop$ into the real interval $[0, 1]$ such that the following axioms hold:

1. $P(W) = 1$ and $P(\emptyset) = 0$ (Normality);
2. $P(\varphi \cup \psi) = (P(\varphi) + P(\psi)) - P(\varphi \cap \psi)$ (Additivity).

These two axioms imply that, where φ and ψ do not overlap, that $P(\varphi \cup \psi) = P(\varphi) + P(\psi)$. They also imply that where $\varphi \subseteq \psi$, that $P(\varphi) \leq P(\psi)$.

The Kolmorgorov axioms are designed with classical logic in mind. In [58], I set out a modified set of axioms that works for models for a wide range of non-classical logics. Where S is the set of situations and P is a function from $Prop$ (the set of propositions on S) into $[0, 1]$, the following are the axioms of this generalised probability theory:

1. $P(S) = 1$ and $P(\emptyset) = 0$;
2. If $\varphi \cup \psi \subseteq \chi$ then $(P(\varphi) + P(\psi)) - P(\varphi \cap \psi) \leq P(\chi)$;
3. If $\chi \subseteq \varphi \cup \psi$ then $(P(\varphi) + P(\psi)) - P(\varphi \cap \psi) \geq P(\chi)$;
4. If $\varphi \subseteq \psi$ then $P(\varphi) \leq P(\psi)$.

Axiom 1 is just Kolmogorov's normality axiom. It is a strange axiom to have in the context of relevant logic. It forces $Prop$ to contain S and $\emptyset$ as propositions. In models that have these as propositions, every proposition entails S and $\emptyset$ entails every proposition. But there is a reason why it is added. If we merely delete axiom 1, then many very weird probability functions become admissible. For example, the function P such that $P(\varphi) = 1$ for all φ and the function $P'(\varphi) = 0$ for all φ would be allowed.

Axioms 2 and 3 are designed especially for logical systems like linear logic that do not treat disjunction in terms of union. In models in which $Prop$ is closed under union, we can derive Kolmorgorov's additivity axiom from axioms 2 and 3. As I say earlier, axiom 4 is derivable in the classical theory, but it is not derivable from axioms 1 to 3 where $Prop$ is not closed under classical relative complement. Axiom 4 is the monotonicity axiom; it is quite intuitive: if ψ is true in all the cases in which φ is true, then ψ must be at least as probable as φ.

As I say in Section 6.1, one of the virtues of probability theory is that it comes packaged with a theory of updating. Let's revert for a minute to the classical theory. Suppose that an agent has a probability function over the set of propositions. He learns something new (φ) and attributes to it the probability 1. Updating on this, for any proposition ψ is given by the following equation:

$$P_{New}(\psi) = \frac{P_{Old}(\psi \cap \varphi)}{P_{Old}(\varphi)}$$

If the probability of the new evidence is not one, then things become rather more complicated. Keeping with the classical theory, what we do is calculate the update as if the probability of φ is one and then multiply this by what we really think the probability of ϕ is, that is,

$$\frac{P_{Old}(\psi \cap \varphi)}{P_{Old}(\varphi)} \times P_{New}(\varphi).$$

Then we do the same for the probability of $\neg\varphi$ and add them together:

$$P_{New}(\psi) = \left[\frac{P_{Old}(\psi \cap \varphi)}{P_{Old}(\varphi)} \times P_{New}(\varphi) \right] + \left[\frac{P_{Old}(\psi \cap \neg\varphi)}{P_{Old}(\neg\varphi)} \times P_{New}(\neg\varphi) \right]$$

This calculation is made possible from the new probability of φ because the probability of $\neg\varphi$ is just $1 - P(\varphi)$. This is not usually the case with regard to relevant and other logics that have non-classical negations. Thus, the theory of updating has to be modified somewhat:

$$P_{New}(\psi) = \left[\frac{P_{Old}(\psi \cap \varphi)}{P_{Old}(\varphi)} \times P_{New}(\varphi) \right]$$
$$+ \left[\frac{P_{Old}(\psi) - P_{Old}(\psi \cap \varphi)}{1 - P_{Old}(\varphi)} \times (1 - P_{New}(\varphi)) \right]$$

In the classical case, $P_{Old}(\psi \cap \neg\varphi)$ is the old probability assigned to the class of worlds in ψ but not in φ. This is captured in the non-classical case by $P_{Old}(\psi) - P_{Old}(\psi \cap \varphi)$.

One use of these sorts of probability functions is in thinking about situated probabilities. An agent might have reasons to accept one probability function P_s in a situation s and another function P_t in a situation t. We can even use this theory to set probabilities on the set of situations u such that there is some situation t in the proposition φ such that $Rstu$. This sort of probability function can tell us, from the standpoint of a situation s, to what degree the proposition φ carries a proposition ψ (see [56]).

6.3 What CBH Is Meant to Measure

The CBH theory places two measures on a set of propositions based on a set of worlds. The first is the measure of the content of a statement, A, which is $1 - P([\![A]\!])$. This measure is rather nice. It tells us how unusual a world is that makes A true.

To understand the second measure, let us first think of a very simple game. Suppose that Ann chooses a number between 1 and 8 and Bob has to guess what that number is by asking yes-no questions. Here is a simple and effective strategy: Bob splits the numbers into two equal classes – 1-4 and 5-8. Then he asks if the number is in 1-4. When Ann answers 'no', he goes on to ask whether the number is 5 or 6. When Ann again answers 'no', he asks whether the number is 7. Ann then says 'no' and Bob realises that the number is 8. 3 such questions are required to tell what the number is of what Ann has chosen regardless of which number she does choose. Information theorists says that the answer has three bits of information which is determined by the equation $Log_2 8 = 3$ (see §3.3).

Now, suppose that we take a statement A (that has a probability that can be expressed by a rational number) and a set of other statements that have the same probability of A such that they *partition* the set of worlds; that is, their propositions do not overlap and together they occupy every possible world. Then we can set up a guessing game like the one given earlier to guess which statement Ann has in mind (it will be A). The number of sets in this partition is

$$\frac{1}{P([\![A]\!])}.$$

Then, using the same reasoning as given earlier we have as the information content

$$Log_2 \frac{1}{P([\![A]\!])}.$$

The CBH measure is really just a generalisation of the sort of measure given earlier.[21]

---

[21] The CBH measure is just a semantic version of Shanon and Weaver's *entropy*, which understands the information contained in a signal to be measured by the uncertainty of what message is at the source of that signal.

6.4 Which Interpretation of Probability?

The CBH measures deal with how hard it is to find out that a proposition is true, if it is true. What sort of interpretation should be given to the probabilities used? Carnap thinks that the sort of probability is *logical probability* that gives an a priori measure of the degree to which an event is possible. Unfortunately, there does not seem to be a workable theory of logical probability available. So, I will move on to the live options – subjective and objective probabilities. Subjective interpretations of probability hold that probabilities measure strengths of belief. If an agent attributes a probability r to a proposition A then the strength of belief of that agent in A is r. Objective interpretations, such as frequency and propensity theories, understand probabilities in agent-independent ways.

Subjective probabilities make sense in this case if we take very seriously the idea that CBH measures how hard it is for a particular individual to discover that he or she is in a world in which A is true. Objective probabilities make sense if we take a much more externalist view and think of the process as highly idealised, that is, one in which the objective probabilities are known.

Information measures could, however, measure features of propositions other than how hard it is to discover that they are true. One way that information theorists like to explain their measures of information is in terms of the degree to which a proposition's coming true would surprise someone. An information measure determined by a subjective probability function could make this notion rather intuitive. An information measure based on a subject probability function could be a measure of surprise in the guise of the downstream difficulty of integrating a proposition. Let us say that I turn around and see out my office window that there is a tornado in Wellington. My subjective probability of there being a tornado before my turning around was very low. Now, I need to update and to integrate this new belief I will have to change a lot of old beliefs about the safety of my family and home, about what I should do, and about whether I will still be meeting a PhD student this afternoon. On the standard probabilist model of belief, all of this will require a lot of cognitive shifting about of beliefs and, as a result of that, of worries, desires, and plans. This just shows, however, that subjective probabilities vary inversely with the amount of downstream information, but it does not show that the exact measures provided by CBH (or any of the other theories of information) represent difficulties in updating accurately.

Objective probabilities may be used as the basis for a theory of the average amount of surprise attributed to a proposition. This is a notion that is supposedly represented by the notion of *entropy* used in Shannon's theory of information. Perhaps of greater interest in the present context is an idea based on Dretske's theory (see §2.8). On his view, a signal i carries the information that A for an agent if and only if the conditional probability $P(A|i \wedge k)$ is 1, where k is the agent's current knowledge. If we take the probability concerned (as Dretske does [23, p 245]) to be objective probability, then this theory is a theory of what the agent is attuned to in an objective sense – that is, what propositions the agent can grasp as information in a situation. The theory, in effect, treats the agent as a detecting mechanism.

We can use the objective version of CBH, combined with Dretske's theory, to describe how much information is encoded in a signal. A signal i encodes a lot of information if it carries unlikely propositions relative to the knowledge of the agent. The point of using objective probabilities in this regard is to determine objective correlations between the agent's state of knowledge and different signals.

Appealing to either objective or subjective probabilities has a downside. In appealing to subjective probabilities one buys into the probabilist thesis that one should organise one's strengths of beliefs according to the probability calculus and update in accordance with the sorts of conditionalisation discussed in Section 6.2. These two requirements are very onerous. It is difficult to organise and update in this manner. Also, it requires that individuals place probabilities on all propositions. Strict subjectivists claim that there are no rules except those given by the formal probability calculus governing how an individual should assign probabilities to propositions about which there is no empirical data. This can lead to different individuals in very similar circumstances having very different probability functions. The issue concerning objective probability has more to do with finding an interpretation that is viable and fits with the uses I have in mind here. Some form of frequency theory would seem best at first glance, but if one adopt that, one needs to connect frequencies (which have to do with event types) with propositions and one needs to decide whether the frequencies involved are actual, possible, or frequencies that are produced under some sort of ideal circumstances. I do not have the space here to treat these issues.

6.5 Probability as a Guide to Information?

While I am on the topic of quantities of information and their relationship to probability theory, I would like to discuss whether probabilities themselves can be used as the basis of a theory of the availability of information. As can be seen from the discussions in Sections 1 and 2, the notion of the availability of information is very slippery. One might think that we could make this notion more concrete by claiming that a piece of information is available to an agent if and only if he or she can rationally determine that the probability of that piece of information is over some threshold. For example, suppose that I want to determine whether I have the information that there is anyone in the office next to mine. I can hear some noises that seem to come from that office, and I assess that the proposition that the office is occupied has a high degree of probability. On this view, I have this information.

Using probabilities in this manner as a guide to which information is in one's information state has some virtues. First, it avoids the issue with conjunction discussed in Section 1.4. Just because two propositions have reasonably high probability does not entail that their conjunction has a high probability.

Nevertheless, I reject the idea that probabilities alone can be used as a guide to the availability of information. Suppose that you buy a lottery ticket and show it to me and I say

> I have information that this ticket will not win.

Surely no one would think that I have just stated the obvious fact that the probability of that ticket's winning is very low. Rather, it is clear that I am promising you much more than that I am claiming that I have information that this ticket in particular will not win, and that this information is *not* applicable to every other ticket in the lottery. Using the rather vague formulation of Section 1, to count as information a proposition has to appear to be true. Whereas it appears very likely that this lottery ticket will lose, it does not appear true. It will appear true when the winning ticket is announced and the number that appears in the newspaper is distinct from the one on the ticket.

One might reply that it is a *pragmatic implicature* of the statement 'I have information that this ticket will not win' that the speaker has information about that particular ticket that makes it different from other tickets, but that it is not part of the meaning of this statement. I think that this is wrong. Suppose that the speaker said

> I have information that this ticket will not win. And I have information about each other ticket that it will lose too.

This just sounds strange, and seems almost as if the speaker has inconsistent information (if he also has the information that at least one ticket will win). The point, however, is that the implication of the first statement that the speaker has particular information about the ticket in question is not cancelled by the further claim that he has the same information about other tickets. Thus, on the cancellation test, the implication that the speaker has information that singles out the one ticket is semantic rather than pragmatic.

In this, we can see another difference between belief and information. Probability might be a very good guide to what should be included among one's beliefs. Probabilism, which is what this view is called, is a defensible theory of justification. It is not, however, a good theory of the availability of information.

6.6 In Lieu of a Conclusion

In this Element I have tried to do two things. I have attempted both to give a tour of the past and current views on the links between logical theories and the notion of information. I have also used this tour as an opportunity to develop and advance a view of this link that takes misinformation and disinformation to be types of information and uses a relevant logic as a way of understanding and manipulating information. In doing both of these things, I have used information theory to justify the use of a logic (as part of the programme 'what information can do for logic') and used a logical theory to make precise notions involved in a (largely qualitative) theory of information (as part of the programme 'what logic can do for information').

Clearly, there is a lot more to do here. In line with recent developments in epistemic logic, there needs to be a theory of information that is commonly held. Many games, both theoretical and ones that people actually play, involve the distinction between information that is private to individual players and that which is common in the sense of common knowledge. For example, in Texas Hold'em poker, each player has a two card hand and there is a common set of cards available to everyone (the 'flop'). Everyone can see the flop and everyone knows that everyone can see the flop (and so on). In order to repeat the recent successes of epistemic logic in the logic of information (in which common information, say, may be unreliable) we need a theory of common information. This is only one area in which further work is needed. Given the distinction between knowledge, belief, and information, much more work on the relationship between these concepts in the context of a logic that combines doxastic, epistemic, and information theoretic modalities.

Bibliography

[1] Patrick Allo. Logical pluralism and semantic information. *Journal of Philosophical Logic*, 36:659–694, 2007.

[2] Gerard Allwein. A qualitative framework for Shannon information theories. In *NSPW '04: Proceedings of the 2004 Workshop on New Securities Paradigms*, pages 23–31, 2005.

[3] Alan Anderson, Nuel D. Belanp, and J. M. Dunn. *Entailment: Logic of Relevance and Necessity*, volume II. Princeton University Press, Princeton, 1992.

[4] Alan Anderson and Nuel D. Belnap. *Entailment: Logic of Relevance and Necessity*, volume I. Princeton University Press, Princeton, 1975.

[5] Arnon Avron. What is relevance logic? *Annals of Pure and Applied Logic*, 165(1):26–48, 2014.

[6] Alexandru Baltag and Sonja Smets. Conditional doxastic models: A qualitative approach to dynamic belief revision. *Electronic Notes in Theoretical Computer Science*, 165:5–21, 2006.

[7] Jon Barwise. Constraints, channels, and the flow of information. In Peter Aczel, David Israel, Yasuhior Katagiri, and Stanley Peters, editors, *Situation Theory and its Applications*, pages 3–28. CSLI Publications, Stanford, 1993.

[8] Jon Barwise. State spaces, local logics, and non-monotonicity. In Maartin de Rijke and Lawrence Moss, editors, *Logic, Language and Computation*, volume 2, pages 1–20. CSLI, Stanford, 1999.

[9] Jon Barwise and John Perry. *Situations and Attitudes*. MIT Press, Cambridge, MA, 1983.

[10] Jon Barwise and Jeremy Seligman. *Information Flow: The Logic of Distributed Systems*. Cambridge University Press, Cambridge, 2008.

[11] Nuel Belnap. How a computer should think. In G. Ryle, editor, *Contemporary Aspects of Philosophy*, pages 30–55. Oriel Press, Stocksfield, 1977.

[12] Nuel Belnap. A useful 4-valued logic. In J. M. Dunn and G. Epstein, editors, *Modern Uses of Many-Valued Logic*, pages 8–37. Reidel, Dordrecht, 1977.

[13] Ross Brady. A content semantics for quantified relevant logic I. *Studia Logica*, 47:111–127, 1988.

[14] Elisabeth Camp. Why maps are not propositional. In Alex Grzankowski and Michelle Montague, editors, *Non-Propositional Intentionality*, pages 19–45. Oxford University Press, Oxford, 2018.

[15] Rudolf Carnap and Yohoshua Bar Hillel. An outline of a theory of semantic information. Technical Report 247, MIT Research Laboratory of Electronics, 1952.

[16] Brian Chellas. Basic conditional logic. *Journal of Philosophical Logic*, 4:133–153, 1975.

[17] Brian Chellas. *Modal Logic: An Introduction.* Cambridge University Press, Cambridge and New York, 1980.

[18] Andy Clark and David Chalmers. The extended mind. *Analysis*, 58:7–19, 1998.

[19] Stephen A. Cook and Robert A. Reckhow. The relative efficiency of propositional proof systems. *The Journal of Symbolic Logic*, 44:36–50, 1979.

[20] M.J. Cresswell. *Structured Meanings.* MIT Press, Cambridge, MA, 1985.

[21] Zoltan Dienes and Josef Perner. A theory of implicit and explicit knowledge. *Behavioral and Brain Sciences*, 22:735–808, 1999.

[22] Kosta Došen. Sequent systems and groupoid models. II. *Studia Logica*, 48:41–65, 1989.

[23] Fred Dretske. *Knowledge and the Flow of Information.* MIT Press, Cambridge, MA, 1981.

[24] J. Michael Dunn. Star and perp. *Philosophical Perspectives*, 7:331–357, 1993.

[25] J. Michael Dunn. The concept of information and the development of modern logic. In W. Stelzner and M. Stoeckler, editors, *Zwischen traditioneller und moderner Logik: Nichtklassiche Ansätze*, pages 423–447. Mentis Verlag GmbH, Paderborn, 2001.

[26] J. Michael Dunn. Contradictory information: Too much of a good thing. *Journal of Philosophical Logic*, 39:425–452, 2010.

[27] J. Michael Dunn. Natural language versus formal language. In Hitoshi Omori and Heinrich Wansing, editors, *New Essays on Belnap-Dunn Logic*, pages 13–20. Springer Verlag, Cham, Switzerland, 2019. Originally presented at an American Philosophical Association meeting in 1968.

[28] J. Michael Dunn and Nicholas M. Kiefer. Contradictory information: Better than nothing? the paradox of the two firefighters. In Can Başkent and Thomas Macaulay Ferguson, editors, *Graham Priest on Dialetheism and Paraconsistency*, pages 231–247. Springer Verlag, 2019.

[29] Luis Estrada-González. Complement-topoi and dual intuitionistic logic. *Australasian Journal of Logic*, 9:26–44, 2010.

[30] Luciano Floridi, editor. *Philosophy of Computing and Information.* Blackwell, Oxford, 2004.

[31] Luciano Floridi. The logic of being informed. *Logique et analyse*, 196:433–460, 2006.

[32] Luciano Floridi. *The Philosophy of Information*. Oxford University Press, Oxford, 2013.

[33] Gottlob Frege. On sense and reference. *The Philosophical Review*, 57:209–230, 1948.

[34] André Fuhrmann. Theory contraction through base contraction. *Journal of Philosophical Logic*, 20(2):175–203, 1991.

[35] P. Gärdenfors. *Knowledge in Flux. Modelling the Dynamics of Epistemic States*. MIT Press, 1988.

[36] Peter Gärdenfors and David Makinson. Revisions of knowledge systems using epistemic entrenchment. In Moshe Vardi, editor, *Proceedings of the Second Conference on Theoretical Aspects of Reasoning about Knowledge*, pages 83–95. Morgan Kaufmann, 1988.

[37] James J. Gibson. *The Ecological Approach to Visual Perception*. Psychology Press, New York, 2015. Originally published in 1979.

[38] Robert Goldblatt. Semantic analysis of orthologic. *Journal of Philosophical Logic*, 3:19–35, 1974.

[39] Robert Goldblatt. *Logics of Time and Computation*. CSLI Publications, 1992.

[40] Paul Grice. *Studies in the Way of Words*. Harvard University Press, Cambridge, MA, 1989.

[41] Jaakko Hintikka. *Logic, Language-Games and Information: Kantian Themes in the Philosophy of Logic*. Oxford, England: Oxford, Clarendon Press, 1973.

[42] I. L. Humberstone. Operational semantics for positive R. *Notre Dame Journal of Formal Logic*, 29:61–80, 1987.

[43] Stanisław Jaśkowski. Rachunek zdań dla systemów dedukcyjnych sprzecznych. *Studia Soc. Scient. Torunensis*, 1:57–77, 1948.

[44] Stanisław Jaśkowski. O koniunkcji dyskusyjnej w rachunku zdań dla systemów dedukcyjnych sprzecznych. *Studia Soc. Scient. Torunensis*, 1:171–172, 1949.

[45] Stanisław Jaśkowski. Propositional calculus for contradictory deductive systems. *Studia Logica*, 24:143–160, 1969. Originally presented in 1948.

[46] Jeffrey C. King. *The Nature and Structure of Content*. Oxford University Press, Oxford, 2007.

[47] Jan Krajíček. *Proof Complexity*. Cambridge University Press, Cambridge, 2019.

[48] Angelika Kratzer. An investigation of the lumps of thought. *Linguistics and Philosophy*, 12:607–653, 1989.

[49] Frederick W. Kroon. Causal descriptivism. *Australasian Journal of Philosophy*, 65:1–17, 1987.

[50] C.I. Lewis and C.H. Langford. *Symbolic Logic*. Dover, New York, second edition, 1959.

[51] Leonard Linsky. *Oblique Contexts*. University of Chicago Pres, Chicago, 1983.

[52] Shay Allen Logan. Depth relevance and hyperformalism. *Journal of Philosophical Logic*, 51:721–737, 2022.

[53] Penelope Maddy. *Second Philosophy*. Oxford University Press, Oxford, 2007.

[54] Edwin Mares. A star-free semantics for R. *Journal of Symbolic Logic*, 60:579–590, 1995.

[55] Edwin Mares. *Relevant Logic: A Philosophical Interpretation*. Cambridge University Press, 2004.

[56] Edwin Mares. Relevant logic, probabilistic information, and conditionals. *Logique et analyse*, 49:399–411, 2006.

[57] Edwin Mares. General information in relevant logic. *Synthese*, 167:343–362, 2009.

[58] Edwin Mares. Belief revision, probabilism, and logic choice. *Review of Symbolic Logic*, 7(4):647–670, 2014.

[59] Edwin Mares and André Fuhrmann. A relevant theory of conditionals. *Journal of Philosophical Logic*, 24:645–665, 1995.

[60] Edwin Mares, Jeremy Seligman, and Greg Restall. Situations, constraints, and channels. In Johan van Benthem and Alice G.B. ter Meulen, editors, *Handbook of Logic and Language*, pages 329–344. Elsevier, Amsterdam, 2010.

[61] Maricarmen Martinez and Sebastian Sequoiah-Grayson. Logic and Information. In Edward N. Zalta, editor, *The Stanford Encyclopedia of Philosophy*. Metaphysics Research Lab, Stanford University, Spring 2019 edition, 2019.

[62] Manuel A. Martins and Igor Sedlár, editors. *Dynamic Logic: New Trends and Applications*, Cham, 2020. Springer Verlag.

[63] Chris Mortensen. *Inconsistent Mathematics*. Kluwer, Dordrecht, 1995.

[64] Ruth Nelson. What is a secret and what does it have to do with computer security? In *Proceedings of the 1994 Workshop on New Securities Paradigms*, pages 74–79, 1994.

[65] Hiroakira Ono. Semantics for substructural logics. In Kosta Došen and Peter Schröder-Heister, editors, *Substructural Logics*, pages 259–291. Oxford University Press, Oxford, 1993.

[66] Francesco Paoli. *Substructural Logics: A Primer*. Springer Verlag, Dordrecht, 2002.

[67] Rohit Parikh. Knowledge and the problem of logical omniscience. In Zibignew Ras and Maria Zemankova, editors, *Proceedings of the Second International Symposium on Intelligent Systems*, pages 432–439. North Holland, Amsterdam, 1989.

[68] Vaughan Pratt. Semantical considerations on the Floyd-Hoare logic. *Proceedings of the 17th Annual IEEE Symposium on Foundations of Computer Science*, 1976.

[69] Graham Priest. *An Introduction to Non-Classical Logic: From If to Is*. Cambridge University Press, Cambridge, second edition, 2008.

[70] Graham Priest. Logical theory choice. *Australasian Journal of Logic*, 16:283–297, 2019.

[71] Vit Punčochář, Igor Sedlár, and Andrew Tedder. Relevant propositional dynamic logic. *Synthese*, 3001 forthcoming.

[72] Stephen Read. Necessary truth and proof. *Kriterion: Journal of Philosophy*, 51:47–67, 2010.

[73] Greg Restall. Four-valued semantics for relevant logics (and some of their rivals). *Journal of Philosophical Logic*, 24(2):139–160, 1995.

[74] Greg Restall. Information flow and relevant logics. In Jeremy Seligman and Dag Westerstøahl, editors, *Logic, Language and Computation*, pages 463–477. CSLI Publications, Stanford, 1995.

[75] Greg Restall. Negation in relevant logics (how i stopped worrying and learned to love the Routley star). In Dov Gabbay and Heinrich Wansing, editors, *What is Negation?*, pages 53–76. Kluwer Academic Publishers, 1999.

[76] Richard Routley and Robert K. Meyer. Semantics for entailment. In Hughes Leblanc, editor, *Truth, Syntax, and Modality*. North Holland, Amsterdam, 1973.

[77] Richard Routley, Robert K. Meyer, Ross Brady, and Val Plumwood. *Relevant Logics and their Rivals*. Ridgeview, Atascardero, 1983.

[78] Richard Routley and Val Routley. The semantics of first-degree entailment. *Noûs*, 6:335–395, 1972.

[79] Bertrand Russell. *The Philosophy of Logical Atomism*. Open Court, La Salle, IL, 1985.

[80] Gillian Russell. The justification of the basic laws of logic. *Journal of Philosophical Logic*, 44:793–803, 2015.

[81] Peter Schotch and Raymond Jennings. On detonating. In G. Priest, R. Routley, and J. Norman, editors, *Paraconsistent Logic*, pages 306–327. Philosophia Verlag, Munich, 1989.

[82] Krister Segerberg. Notes on conditional logic. *Studia Logica*, 48:157–168, 1989.

[83] Jeremy Seligman. *Perspectives: A Relativistic Approach to the Theory of Information*. PhD thesis, University of Edinburgh, 1990.

[84] Sebastian Sequoias-Grayson. The scandal of deduction: Hintikka on the information yield of deductive inferences. *Journal of Philosophical Logic*, 37:67–94, 2008.

[85] Claude E. Shannon and Warren Weaver. *The Mathematical Theory of Communication*. University of Illinois Press, Champaign, IL, 1963.

[86] Dan Sperber and Deirdre Wison. *Relevance: Communication and Cognition*. Blackwell, Oxford, second edition, 1995.

[87] Andrew Tedder. Information flow in the vicinity of BB. *The Australasian Journal of Logic*, 18:1–24, 2021.

[88] Andrew Tedder and Marta Bilková. Relevant propositional dynamic logic. *Synthese*, 200(3):1–42, 2022.

[89] Johan van Benthem. *Language in Action: Categories, Lambdas, and Dynamic Logic*. MIT Press, Cambridge, MA, 1995.

[90] Johan van Benthem. *Logical Dynamics of Information and Interaction*. Cambridge University Press, Cambridge, 2011.

[91] Johan van Benthem and David Israel. Review of Jon Barwise and Jeremy Seligman, Information flow. *Journal of Logic, Language, and Information*, 8:390–397, 1999.

[92] Timothy Williamson. Semantic paradoxes and abductive methodology. In *Reflections on the Liar*, pages 325–346. Oxford: Oxford University Press, 2017.

I dedicate this book to the memory of four philosophical friends – Mike Dunn, Bob Meyer, Peter Schotch, and Jill LeBlanc: a teacher, a mentor, a colleague, and a long-time close buddy.

Cambridge Elements ≡

Philosophy and Logic

Bradley Armour-Garb
SUNY Albany

Bradley Armour-Garb is chair and Professor of Philosophy at SUNY Albany. His books include *The Law of Non-Contradiction* (co-edited with Graham Priest and J. C. Beall, 2004), *Deflationary Truth* and *Deflationism and Paradox* (both co-edited with J. C. Beall, 2005), *Pretense and Pathology* (with James Woodbridge, Cambridge University Press, 2015), *Reflections on the Liar* (2017), and *Fictionalism in Philosophy* (co-edited with Fred Kroon, 2020).

Frederick Kroon
The University of Auckland

Frederick Kroon is Emeritus Professor of Philosophy at the University of Auckland. He has authored numerous papers in formal and philosophical logic, ethics, philosophy of language, and metaphysics, and is the author of *A Critical Introduction to Fictionalism* (with Stuart Brock and Jonathan McKeown-Green, 2018).

About the Series

This Cambridge Elements series provides an extensive overview of the many and varied connections between philosophy and logic. Distinguished authors provide an up-to-date summary of the results of current research in their fields and give their own take on what they believe are the most significant debates influencing research, drawing original conclusions.

Cambridge Elements ☰

Philosophy and Logic

Printed in the United States
by Baker & Taylor Publisher Services